This is a clear exploration of many
assume unwittingly in everyday thi
Elspeth Waters, *Journalist*

The factual evidence has been evalı
the hard argumentative female ratio
readers and urges you to read more. Definitely a page turner.
Fatemeh Salehi, *Uxbridge*

A thought provoking insight into logical thinking, written in a witty
and understandable fashion. Definitely opens the mind to alternative
view points. A very interesting and enjoyable read. I look forward to
the next one.
Tracy Fry, *Surrey Quays, London*

Dear Mr. Beckley - Your book "The Red Herring and the Power of
Logic" is a most valuable contribution. I could simply not stop
reading it. The "Ten Commandments" that you mention on page
130 have been part of my basic approach to science and society
since early days. Your book should be translated into Swedish,
and into other languages, because it ought to be part of the
curriculum of high school and university students.
Professor A. Lima-de-Faria, *Lund University, Sweden*

As far as I know little has been written for the lay person recently
about what was seen as a vital subject for all educated people in
the Middle Ages. It still is of course, and needs to come out of the
domain of esoteric philosophy and back where it belongs, as part
of the make-up of ordinary members of a civilised society.
Dr Andrew Lack, *Oxford Brookes University*

It is also beautifully designed and produced: it looks an attractive
book and deserves to sell. It is a pity that I no longer teach the
first-year students because the modules included some logic and I
could have used your book. I know you did not intend it
primarily for college use but I don't know of a better one for the
informal fallacies. I will try to get the library to order a few
copies for general use.
T.Hussey, *Emeritus Professor of Philosophy, Chilterns University*

About the author and illustrator

The illustrator for the book, Shirin Saramad Adl, holds a First Class BA Honours in Illustration from Loughborough University. In 1999 she received the Hallmark M&S division talented designer award at the new designer's exhibition in London.

Colin Beckley is currently reading Philosophy and Anthropology at Brookes University, Oxford.

All quotations printed in the blackboard sketches are taken or adapted from the Sherlock Holmes stories of Sir Arthur Conan Doyle.

THE RED HERRING

COLIN BECKLEY

*This book has been printed digitally and produced in a standard specification
in order to ensure its continuing availability*

Published by Antony Rowe Publishing Services in 2005
48-50 Birch Close
Eastbourne
East Sussex
BN22 6PE

© Colin Beckley 2005

All rights reserved. Unauthorised duplication contravenes
applicable laws.

ISBN 9781905200153

Printed and bound by CPI Antony Rowe, Eastbourne

Acknowledgements

Some years ago in the Cottage Bookshop in Penn I chanced upon a copy of 'Straight and Crooked Thinking' by Robert H. Thouless. Taken by the title I made my purchase of a book that made a great impression upon me as a younger man. The sentiments stayed with me, I was lucky. Many years later, on reflection, I thought it a pity that so few others had shared this advantage as the book was now out of print and out of date with the post-world war 2 examples it employed. The inspiration was not to try and emulate Thouless but to capture the spirit of the book and write something appropriate for the 21st century. None of this would have been possible without the help of the following.

Kay Humphrey's initial help and web designs that accompanied this book were essential. Amber Morton had the unenviable task of deciphering my notes and putting them into type. Shirin Adl Saramad has been so helpful and supportive in addition to being a great illustrator. Jane Brearley volunteered to convert my texts into English and also thankfully challenged some of my original assumptions which led me to much thought, further clarification and changes. Together with Dave Brearley (who cooks a great meal) they make a great team and I am indebted to their help and friendship. Perhaps the most onerous task fell upon Trevor Hussey who carefully put his critical eye over the philosophical aspects. Fortunately his efforts prevented me from going to print with numerous 'clangers' inherent in the original writings. His support and encouragement have been so valuable.Holly Small should not be forgotten in helping to prepare this book for print. Finally I must also thank Nancy Hussey, Roxana Beckley and Elpie Waters for their essential observations.

I dedicate this book to
Maryam, Roxana and Alex.

CONTENTS

I   Introduction

1   PART ONE - Logical thinking
15   PART TWO - Fallacies of Distraction and/or Irrelevance
37   PART THREE - Fallacies of Ambiguity
49   PART FOUR - Fallacies of Definition
60   PART FIVE - Causal and Faulty Inductive Fallacies
75   PART SIX - Formal Logic
110   PART SEVEN - The Threats
124   PART EIGHT - Test Your Reasoning Powers
129   The Ten Commandments
130   Glossary
137   Answers
138   Further Reading

THE RED HERRING AND THE POWER OF LOGIC
Introduction

This book is designed to help people of all persuasions to think more clearly and gain an independence of mind. As we learn the methods of logical thinking we will see many problems or issues in a new light. Our approach to these will gain a new confidence. The gift of independence is there already, waiting to be adopted, absorbed and applied to every day life. It is a gift that cannot be taken away once we have it. It is a gift that will become second nature and one will wonder how one ever managed without it.

In fact we have the gift of independence within us, ready to flourish, awaiting the spark that will set us on course. Regretfully there are influences that inhibit our logical reasoning powers and prevent us from gaining fully independent thinking. Fortunately however, humans are naturally curious of mind and by engaging with this book you have already taken the first steps towards identifying these preventive forces. We often encounter the arguments of authorities and even friends that sound a little suspect but we can't put our finger on exactly why.

In books on logical or critical reasoning one often comes across advice on how to 'win' an argument or how to persuade and influence others. It suggests a rather combative approach. Businessmen and women are encouraged to spot fallacies in their opponents' arguments but discussions and arguments are then seen as competitions with winners and losers.

This is not the approach that I wish to support. I heartily accept that the 'best argument wins the day'. One must remember though that the best argument may not be one's own. Recognising this is important because we are tempted to lose sight of the truth, in order to get one's own point across. We all like to have the final say. We get a buzz from feeling that we have impressed someone with our convincing arguments.

If we look at the world we can see where this type of thought manifests itself and leads unfortunately to illogical and dishonest reasoning. All too often, the party politician constructs arguments that 'appeal' to an intended audience. Lawyers and barristers often construct defence and cross-examination strategies. In both cases there is no genuine enquiry into the truth, only a desire to convince people by means of any sophistry available. It is not uncommon that newspaper editors deliberately distort or withhold information to satisfy a readership with pre-conceived opinions. Religious leaders, with rare exception try to restrict the free flow of information and criticism of their beliefs. They insist on faith and an unquestioning attitude. They assume the truth.

To the logical thinker, however, these assumptions cannot be made. Truth is recognised as desirable and yet difficult to achieve. If we are to have any success then the logical thinker must approach all the relevant information with an open mind. Our reasoning must be sound and we must free ourselves from trying to impress others. None of these requirements are easy, but they are a beginning.

We must look for consistency. Where there is want of it we must suspect deception.

PART ONE
Logical thinking

Very few people today would be able to give an accurate description of what a logical person is, and an even smaller number of people would be able to say what the benefits of logical thinking are.

Many, if they have watched the popular 60s science fiction series, Star Trek, would conjure a picture of Mr Spock, the Vulcan with the funny shaped ears. He could provide cold and dispassionate answers to Captain Kirk's questions that seemed to contain profound insights that mere humans had overlooked. Indeed, Mr Spock added logical insights that somehow seemed to transcend those of his other colleagues on board the Enterprise.

Others may imagine the logician as the sort of person who buys a book of logic problems before embarking upon a summer vacation. They then proceed to bury their heads within, whilst everyone else is swimming in the sea or playing beach volleyball. This stereotyped person in their professional life would probably be a computer expert, who spends hours at the screen. When required they could, diagnose exactly why it is that your computer has crashed. Furthermore, they could even supply you with a floppy disk that they have written themselves. Unknown to us, this is written in a mathematical logic, and when inserted in the slot puts everything on the computer back in order again.

For our purpose, however, neither of these possible images will suit. The type of informal logic this book deals with has little to do with the emotionless Mr Spock or the computer mathematical whiz kid.

What is Logical Thinking?

To answer this question clearly, it may be best to say what logical thinking is not concerned with. There are many misconceptions, as illustrated earlier, that need dispelling. Logic is not about choice or how to make choices. It cannot tell you which coat to buy, which wine to drink or which foods are best to eat. Moreover, logic has nothing to say about which friends you should choose or which school or college to attend, or even which career to pursue (if any).

Logic is not about moral or ethical choices or guidance. Being logical will not tell us what we ought or ought not to do. It won't tell us what is 'good' behaviour and what is 'bad' behaviour, or whether we have certain 'rights' and 'duties'. This is for the moral philosopher to answer, or at least attempt to answer.

Logic is not about being emotionless or without a sense of humour. Despite the portrayal of our Vulcan friend, people can enjoy a joke, have fun, display human emotions and still be logical. There is nothing illogical about having a good cry if there is something upsetting. Nor is there anything illogical about laughing at a good joke. To try or to pretend otherwise could be to deny our nature.

Logic is not gender specific. It is something of a myth to think that 'men are more logical that women'. Either sex has the potential to develop and improve their logical techniques. There is no gender bias. If anyone should doubt this, it should be pointed out that several of the leading authorities on logic as an academic study during the last half-century have been female.

At this point one is quite entitled to be asking oneself 'what exactly is this logic and is it of any value?' In some ways 'logic' can be viewed in the same way that education has been viewed in the past. Those that didn't have the benefit of an 'education' were unable to see the benefits of it.

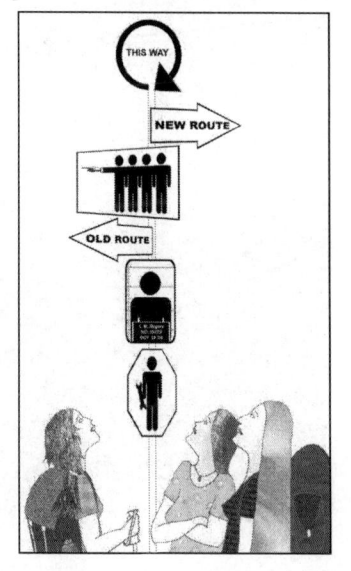

Similarly with logic, once you have become familiar with the reasoning techniques it is unlikely that you will not find them useful, or that you would wish to discard your newly developed mental abilities. I say 'developed' because most of us are inherently logical but to varying degrees. To some it comes easily and they will feel that they have such capacities and that they are already employed but without a formal recognition. To others, logical reasoning will be seen as more difficult to comprehend and employ. As we read through the book we will learn to identify beliefs or opinions that are the result of fallacious arguments. In society today we often come across people who accept these unsupported conclusions as 'normal' or 'natural.' As we unravel these we will begin to appreciate a greater sense of the mind's independence. To arrive at one's own independent opinions, freed from badly reasoned techniques, and to arrive in as unbiased a manner as is humanly possible, is something special. This should not be underestimated and yet is difficult to describe as an experience.

So far, I have not said what this logic or logical reasoning actually is. We have merely been skirting around the subject, hopefully with curiosity aroused, but without answers. Following on from the previous paragraph one could define logic as 'the study of correct reasoning and sound argument.' It is not the psychological study of how people actually reason or argue, it is how they ought to argue.

The best way to describe this intangible subject is with the use of analogy. Let us imagine that we are travellers who wish to reach an unfamiliar destination – Place X. We have no guide, map or compass to instruct us. To conclude our journey successfully in the shortest, most direct route, we are forced to seek the help of others.

But how can we be sure that the advice we receive is reliable? If the journey is a crucial one, then acting on bad advice could prove fatal. If the journey is less crucial, then acting on bad advice could still be very inconvenient. So what tools do we have at our disposal to evaluate whether the advice we receive is good?

This is where logic comes in. Logic has nothing to say about whether you ought to go to Place X, but it can be used as a tool to examine whether the advice you receive is reasoned correctly. Further, logic will enable you to decide whether the advice received will help you reach your chosen destination. Continuing with our analogy, on the journey we will meet several people who are willing to direct us but their directions may sound a little suspect.

For example, one person asserts that we need to travel due north and is quite certain about this, but the person then points in a direction that is due south! We reason that this must be wrong because of the position of the sun. They have given us contrary advice.

Another person offers advice that sends us round in circles and we get no further. Another boasts that we should listen to him as he is a travel writer, but then we discover that he has never been to our destination. Others try to deliberately trick us and prevent us from concluding our journey, and some others, although very kind and considerate, innocently send us in the wrong direction because they themselves have little idea.

The purpose of logic in this book is to identify those arguments that may lead us astray. These arguments that are reasoned incorrectly are commonly known as 'fallacies'. The people we encounter on our journey through life will at some stage offer advice and arguments to support their advice. Logical thinking will help us determine which advice is reasoned well and whether we reach the correct conclusions. Before we examine these fallacies more thoroughly we must be aware of some deceptions that may divert us from the task at hand.

Emotive Words and Euphemisms

You see, but you do not observe

One method of misleading people that is prevalent throughout society is the use of emotive words and euphemisms (substitution of mild for blunt expression). These can be either innocently or deliberately deployed.

Typical of the worst offenders are newspapers, politicians and the military (see the table of military euphemisms). In every day parlance they are also used regularly, for they are difficult to avoid and we are all guilty to some extent.

Emotive words and euphemisms are frequently used to evoke a desired emotion in the listener. The perpetrator is probably either putting a gloss on a situation or conversely making a situation sound worse than it actually is. For example in the 1980s Margaret Thatcher was Prime Minister in the UK. She made a speech and famously said that the 'lady was not for turning'. This meant that she was committed to the policies her government wished to pursue and would not reverse their decisions. This was conveyed to the public in two broad ways. Newspapers that were pro Conservative and supported her, described her as 'courageous', 'determined', 'brave', 'committed'. Conversely, those papers that were not supporters of the Conservatives described her actions as 'Stubborn,' 'single minded', obstinate and as someone whose mind was closed to 'evidence'.

The ambition of the anti-Thatcher press was to portray an unfavourable perspective on her actions whilst the Conservative press attempted to present a positive

perspective. Sometimes neutral words are difficult to find and one unwittingly slips into the usage of emotive words. There is remedy when such neutral words are hard to find, one could describe a situation such as the Margaret Thatcher example as follows,

"The Prime Minister vowed not to reverse her policies, this was widely applauded as a sign of firm government by her supporters in the party and the Conservative press, but her actions were not well received by the opposition who described her as stubborn".

This paragraph is a better approach and more objective because it conveys the range of opinions used to describe the Prime Minister's actions. The listener can then make up one's own mind about the events and judge the situation on the reasons given for the actions by the Prime Minister. Logic, however will not be able to tell you which reasons are the best ones, it can only alert you to the possible dangers of the employment of emotive words. A good exercise is to take a daily newspaper and search through a few news issues identifying emotive language.

It is good to know which newspapers support which parties and recognizing the use of emotive words will soon indicate their alignments. Be careful however not to fall into the trap of dismissing opinions simply because they are written in those newspapers that do not support your political views.

Each of the media statements above commit to the fallacy of, *ad hominem* argumentation (see page 15)

Euphemisms-Some Examples

From the military

Air support = attacking enemy by means of aircraft dropping bombs
To deliver = to drop on an enemy, esp. bombs
Delivery vehicle = a missile that carries a bomb
Intervention = military invasion
Incident = a battle in peacetime
Neutralize = kill (CIA MANUAL 2000)
Pre emptive strike = an unprovoked attack without warning
To terminate/liquidate eliminate = to kill
Combat fatigue = shell shock (now post-traumatic stress disorder)
Laying down a carpet = saturation bombing
Collateral casualties = civilian deaths during bombing raids or other military operations.

Incontinent ordance, (Friendly fire) = mistaken shelling of one's own troops
Assertive disarmament = destruction of the enemy's fire power

From Commerce

Income protection – tax avoidance
Negative growth – decline
Natural break – interventions of adverts on TV
Price revisions – price increase
In retailing all adjustments and revisions need euphemisms when the price increases, but there is no need for euphemisms when the price decreases.
Downsizing – sacking staff
Rationalizing – sacking staff.

Evasive ploys in Conversation – Flippancy

This ploy is employed when someone purposely introduces a humorous comment in order to subvert the discussion from the main point.

Some years ago I remember taking part in a debate about human nature, which ran along the familiar 'nature versus nurture' divide. One of the speakers argued in favour of nurture. She said people had more chance of developing their capacities if they were brought up in an environment that provided good housing, education, healthy food and supportive peers. She then used an analogy, that if one were in the garden and bringing on plants from seeds one is more likely to be successful if the soil is good, the seed is fed and watered regularly and protection is provided from the elements. If one neglected this nurturing then the plant was less likely to flourish and may even not survive, all other things being equal.

So far a strong argument. However all her reasoned points were lost when a member of the group opposing her view said, "I'm a gardener and my plants do well because I surround them with horse shit!" To which the group broke into laughter and the conversation became fragmented.

These ploys are difficult to expose at the time of conversation. If one could think quickly it could be pointed out that the person who interjected with the joke contradicted himself. For he himself practised nurturing in his own garden.

Evasive ploys in Conversation – Asking for Definitions

Once again in conversations where there are opposing views another trick is sometimes deployed. Consider the following.

In a debate one person was arguing that the democracies in the west should not supply weapons to dictatorships in the developing world. An opponent of this view, rather than giving reasons for supplying such weapons diverted the conversation by asking, "what do you consider to be a democracy, how do you define it?"

The debate then took the route of jostling between the virtues of Ancient Greek Democracy and representative democracy etc. The original point about supplying weapons was lost. Once again in conversations it is difficult to steer the debate back to the original topic. One also has to be careful because sometimes it is quite legitimate to ask for the definition of a term, if that term is ambiguous or one is unclear about what the speaker is referring to. For example, if someone said 'I don't believe in equality' it would be good to discover what he or she means. A definition is in order. Does one mean equality between the sexes? Equality before the law? Equality of pay or equal opportunity? Such a definition is necessary when someone utters vague ideas.

What is a fallacy?

During the course of our lives we will meet a variety of people with a variety of opinions. Some of these opinions could contradict each other. For example, people might be for or against foxhunting. As logicians we will not say if foxhunting is right or wrong but we can examine the reasoning behind these conclusions.

If a conclusion is not supported by the correct form of reasoning then a fallacy has been committed. Fallacies take many forms, the earliest being identified over two thousand years ago by the Greek philosopher Aristotle. It is quite remarkable that Aristotle's identifications still hold true today. In medieval times Aristotle's works were closely studied and you will notice that many of the forthcoming fallacies have Latin names. It is not important to remember all the names but it is valuable to understand why fallacies have been committed.

I have updated a large selection of these fallacies by introducing contemporary examples from every day life and conversation. Unfortunately there is no particular methodology for learning these fallacies but as you read through, their nature will become apparent.

Some fallacies are blatantly obvious, and yet commonly held. Others are much more subtle and it is harder to understand why they are fallacies. Hopefully I can make this transparent. We must remember also that in everyday speech the word 'fallacy' is applied loosely to factual errors. In our study however, we will be concerned with the meaning of 'fallacy' in the context of logical argument i.e. does the conclusion follow on from the premise? We must further be aware that when we forthwith talk of arguments we will not be referring to 'mud slinging,' 'slanging matches' or 'rows.' Logical arguments are seen in a dispassionate light and are therefore considered more likely to secure the truth.

Traditionally, fallacies have fallen into two broad categories, informal and formal. We are mostly concerned with the former but some consideration is given to formal logic in the later chapters. Informal fallacies have proved a problem for logicians to classify. To date there is no consensus on defining the criteria for these groupings and on deciding which particular fallacies fall into which particular grouping. However, this should not deter us, as overriding importance will be placed on understanding why a fallacy has been committed and how we might avoid making the same mistakes. Based on certain similarities I have grouped the fallacies into four main divisions:

1. Distraction or Irrelevance
2. Ambiguity
3. Definition
4. Casual and Faulty Induction.

Before you embark upon reading the various fallacies write down (and retain) on a piece of paper 4 reasons why you either support foxhunting or why you support a ban. If you are non-committal upon this subject then choose 4 reasons to support a belief you hold that has opposing views from other people.

A warning for those who seek security in strong or firm beliefs: reading this book might make you question a lot of fundamental ideas you may hold. I am not saying that you will change your beliefs; you may retain them. Whichever course you take I am confident that you will appreciate them, the old and the new, as your own, and not foisted upon you by someone else.

Singularity is almost invariably a clue. The more and featureless and commonplace a fallacy is, the more difficult it is to bring it home.

PART TWO
Fallacies of Distraction and/or Irrelevance

These are the fallacies that we are most likely to encounter in everyday life. As the names suggest the arguments are either an intentional or unintentional distraction from the point of issue. Typical of this is the infamous 'Red Herring ' fallacy.

Under examination we will discover why the reasons put forward to support a particular conclusion are not relevant but highly deceptive.

Argumentum ad hominem

This literally means argument directed at the man but of course it could also be directed against a woman.

Examples

'How can you give any moral guidance, I've seen you reading pornography'

Or

'Don't ask her for political advice on voting, she used to be an Anarchist.'

This is a very common form of fallacy that attempts to undermine a person's view or argument by attacking, not the argument, but the person themselves. It is a tactic used particularly by newspaper editors, who 'dig the dirt' on a politician they wish to discredit. Once the politician is discredited then their ideas or arguments are usually undervalued or discarded.

This method of discrediting someone or something can also be employed when appealing to certain circumstances.

For example

'I don't see why you can't accept the expansion of the road system, after all you own and drive a car everyday.'

Or

'Of course you're against positive discrimination, you're white.'

Sometimes it is right to refer to the circumstances of an individual or organisation that is making a claim. Consider the millions of pounds that were spent on research by tobacco companies to show that tobacco doesn't harm people. Was this research used to establish the truth of the matter or to preserve the financial ambitions of the corporations concerned?

Tip: Try to think if the truth or falsity of the issue is related in any way to the circumstances or character of the person or organisation putting forward the attack.

Argumentum ad hominem tu quoque

This form of personal attack adds to the sting that the person does not practise what they preach.

Examples

'You know old Mr Boozalot is hardly ever sober, well he had the cheek to say I shouldn't drink.'

'He said I wasn't keeping the kitchen clean enough but you should see how his garage looks.'

'She advocates that we should vote green but she never recycles her bottles.'

Once again the proponent is undermining the character of the person rather than the issue itself. 'Recycling', 'drinking' and 'being tidy' are all issues that should be judged on their own merits and not because the proponent fails to apply them in their own routines.

Tip: Try to divorce the issue from the person

Argumentum ad antiquitatem

Appeal to Age or Custom

Example

'Religious ideas have always been with us since time immemorial. Can any one doubt their truth in consideration of all the persecution they have received?'

Or

'If we change our currency (from the pound) we will lose part of our heritage.'

This type of argument rests on the idea that if something has been around for a long time it must have some value, otherwise we would have discarded it. However, the idea that the world was flat existed for many years and further wasn't it also the case that non-believers, pagans etc were (and still are) persecuted for their beliefs? So just because something has been around for years this is not sufficient reason for believing it is a good thing.

Tip: If you think a custom or something of antiquity is of value try to give other reasons why you believe this, rather than just rely on the fact that it is old.

Ignoratio elenchi

Irrelevant conclusion

Examples

'We ought to accept Genetically Modified food into this country because if we don't it will be a victory for Greenpeace and the politics of civil disobedience.'

'If you look around the world all the disadvantaged people turn to religion to alleviate their unfortunate circumstances. From this experience the existence of God cannot be doubted.'

'There is nothing morally wrong with eating meat, if we didn't eat beef for example, then cows would become an extinct species.'

'If this country doesn't go ahead and supply the dictatorship of General Galterai with missiles then another European country will only step in and fulfil the order.'

This is a frequent tactic, especially amongst politicians. When a conclusion cannot be supported with good reasons an irrelevant argument that may appeal to the listeners is employed. The debate concerning GM foods should be conducted over considerations of our health and the effects on Agriculture, not on the possible success for Greenpeace.

Tip: This argument takes the form 'p is true therefore q is true'. You have to show that p and q are quite distinct.

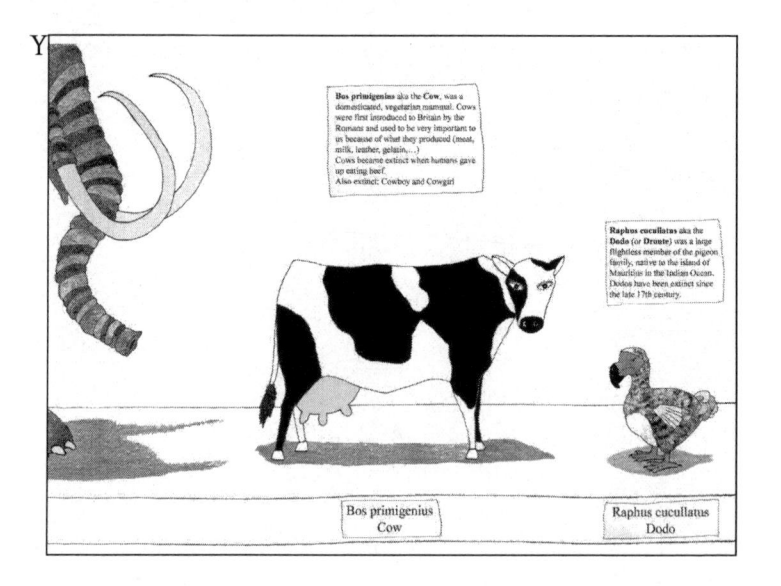

Argumentum ad baculum

Appeal to Force

Examples

'All non believers will spend an eternity in the burning fires of hell'

'Any employees that do not accept the conclusions of the company review could find themselves seeking new employment'

'If she continues to perform experiments on animals we have every moral right to carry out measures that will damage her home and family'

PART TWO - Fallacies of Distraction and/or Irrelevance

Authorities that do not wish to enter into a rational debate commonly use this device. It is less of an argument and more of a threat. A curious variation of this form of persuasion occurred during the 1980s when the government was pushing forward with unpopular economic policies. They argued that we have to take our medicine, (even if we don't like its taste), if we are going to achieve economic success.

Another similar example is the expression sometimes heard, 'you have to be cruel to be kind'. Both this and the previous argument suggest that some form of hardship or suffering inflicted will be beneficial in the long term for those on the receiving end. One is a little sceptical though and it is worth asking if this is simply a way of stifling debate and allowing badly thought out ideas to continue without discussion.

It has been tactical amongst some animal rights protesters to threaten researchers who experiment on animals. Whatever one thinks of the morality behind such actions their argument cannot be established or supported by such dangerous intimidation. In order to validate their conclusions they must give reasons and evidence. (If they do not they are in danger of alienating any public support that may exist for their alternative ideas.)

Tip: Try not to devalue your own arguments and opinions by recourse to threats or intimidation. If your arguments are sufficiently strong they will not require this device.

21

Argumentum ad crumenam

Wisdom of the wealthy

Examples

'If you're so smart, why aren't you rich?'

'See that guy over there, he oozes with money, just look at that car and his designer suit, you can see he's no fool.'

This type of view suggests that successful people with money can speak with more authority than those with less money. So, the richer one is the more likely one is to be correct. It is difficult to see how gaining wealth for instance necessarily involves gaining knowledge. People can gain wealth by lucky circumstances; they could inherit a large fortune, have a lucky break on the lottery or become successful by virtue of their appearance or because of a particular talent that is rewarded by demand in our economic market. It doesn't follow that these financially successful people are necessarily wiser or become wiser as they grow richer.

Tip: Ask yourself what things makes one wiser?

Advertisers are well aware of our psychological weaknesses when we value wealth. People frequently believe that expensive commodities are superior to cheap commodities. This has been demonstrated by tests where, for example in the case of washing powders, people were asked to test and grade three different powders: A, B, C, where A is the cheapest and in the plainest of cartons and C is the most expensive and in the most prestigious looking carton. Unsurprisingly the majority of people said that C the expensive powder gave the best results and A the cheapest was reported the worst performer. This is curious because what the participants didn't know was that the powder within each box was the same (apart from some irrelevant changes to the colour).

So be careful, the most expensive is not always the best and the cheapest is not always the worst. Try to judge things on their merits and not on the packaging. The same principle applies to statements put forward by others.

Argumentum ad ignorantiam

'Argument from ignorance'

Examples

'Of course God exists. No one can prove otherwise'

'How do you know that plants don't think?'

'Of course God doesn't exist. No one can prove otherwise'.

'Stonehenge was built by Aliens.'

'Not a single flying saucer (UFO) report has been authenticated. Therefore, we may assume there are no such things as UFOs.

'There is no evidence that monkeys feel pain, they may exhibit pain behaviour but as they have no consciousness, they feel no pain.'

A person employing this tactical argument is shifting the burden of proof on to you and getting a proof in such circumstances is probably impossible. Remember though because you can't disprove X it doesn't follow that X is true. All that follows is that X is unproven. Lets suppose someone puts forward the negative statement 'Yeties do not exist.' This statement could be disproved if we discovered such a creature in the Himalayas, for example. A negative statement can always be disproved by a positive result. However, when we look at positive statements, such as, 'Yeties exist,' then we can see that positive statements can never be fully disproved because there is always a chance that we may discover a Yeti in the future!

Tip: In the end you will have to weigh up the evidence for each claim and base your opinion on which you think is the more plausible. Or you could also say, 'I don't have enough evidence to form an opinion yet. I remain open-minded.'

Argumentum ad Lazarum

Appeal to poverty

Examples

'Priest and Nuns are more likely to possess insight into the meaning of life because they have given up the distractions of wealth.'

'Hermits are wise, they are not distracted by possessions'

'At that price you can't go wrong'

'Responsible breeders don't make money'

'Father Jones has taken a vow of poverty, therefore he has the truth'.

'The Pope lives a simple, austere life, so he must be more spiritually attuned to the hearts of people.'

This fallacy is the opposite of the earlier one *Argumentum ad crumenam*. Instead of an appeal to the wealth of a person or the economic value of an artifact the appeal is now to poverty. It's the idea that if one gives up material wealth then one is unburdened by it and can therefore make objective or impartial views.

Poverty may give valuable insights into the unfortunate plights of some people but it's difficult to see how it would help us decide on a lot of issues, such as, 'Is abortion permissible?', 'Should we eat meat?'. 'Does the World Bank advantage or disadvantage the underdeveloped world?' Poverty offers no special insights into these matters and neither does wealth.

Tip: Ask yourself if poverty or wealth has any bearing on the issue in question.

Argumentum ad novitatem

Argument for modernity, newness

Examples

'Vote New Labour'

'You ought to buy this as it's the latest fashion'

'This motor is superior to others because it has the latest designs'

In the field of advertising, the word 'new' is regarded as an eye catcher as it plays upon and raises our natural curiosity. As you can see from above, politicians are also not averse to using this technique in order to influence people. Implicit is the idea that newness or modernity is an improvement upon what has gone before. It is the opposite of the *Argumentum antiquitatem* where age or custom is appealed to.

Tip: Consider if the idea or promotion has anything else to recommend it other than the recommendation that it is new.

Argumentum ad nauseum

Argument of repetition

Examples

'Four legs good, two legs bad'

'Drugs are wrong'
(ad nauseam because people are sick of hearing it.)

Politicians, teachers and advertisers commonly use this type of device. George Orwell in his book *Animal Farm* demonstrated how totalitarian regimes attempt to influence (often successfully) their populations. The pigs in the story used the same tricks that Goebbels from Nazi Germany employed in the 1930s. Continuous use of verbal and written slogans, until one becomes sick of hearing them but nevertheless accepts them as true.

Tip: Remember: A repetitious slogan could still be true; you have to decide if it is supported by facts or good reason.

Argumentum ad populum

Emotional appeal – Snob value – Bandwagon

Examples

'Although we do not like to see the erosion of civil liberties, the public sympathises with the government's measures to tackle terrorism.'

'Opinion polls have shown that the Conservatives will win the next election, so you may as well vote for them'

'Sorry, ask anyone...'

It is not only advertisers who routinely use this method of influence, politicians now realise that psychological methods can be more effective than rational arguments. Political parties go out of their way to gain the support, especially in the run up to an election, of popular public celebrities. Several years ago in the UK there was a referendum on our status in the European Community. The 'Yes' camp devoted their political broadcast slots to a stream of well-known public figures outside of politics who simply said, "vote yes to Europe", or words to that effect. It was psychologically convincing. The 'yes' vote won by a large majority, turning over the results of earlier opinion polls that suggested a massive 'No' vote.

Tip: Write down what the arguments are and the reasons to support them. Consider the reasons and try to think of the opposing arguments before deciding which has the stronger case.

Argumentum ad verecundiam

Appeal to inappropriate authority.

Examples

'Isaac Newton was a genius and he believed in God'

'Dr Wiseman studied for years at college and medical school and she says its wrong to eat meat'

'Even the Prime Minister thinks Chelsea will win the cup final.'

In such cases as these the proponent of a view is trying to bolster their argument by appealing to an authority.

Sometimes it is legitimate to quote an authority as evidence for an argument. If someone has studied for years in a particular area of research then it often pays to listen to what they have to say. Whereas, the Prime Minister may know a lot about international affairs but he or she probably knows little more than anyone else about Chelsea's fortunes in the forthcoming cup final.

Tip: Be careful when you wish to add evidence to support your view, sometimes there is controversy from within a scientific community. Try to get evidence from both viewpoints first.

It is often useful to distinguish between someone being in authority and someone as an authority. Being in authority does not guarantee that that person's opinion is worthy of respect.

Straw man

Examples

'We should bring back conscription. People don't want to join the military because they find it an inconvenience. But they should realize that there are more important things than convenience.'

'You say that you support Prison reform and shorter sentencing. But if we make prisons like holiday camps how will that deter potential criminals.'

'We all know that communism doesn't work so why argue for a fairer division of wealth.'

PART TWO - Fallacies of Distraction and/or Irrelevance

In the straw man fallacy a false representation of a view is put forward and then attacked, conveniently side stepping the original point. Supporting a fairer division of wealth does not necessarily involve communism, one could be a liberal, social democrat or a socialist. The arguer invokes communism because they feel it is a softer target.

Similarly, someone supporting Prison Reform is not thinking of providing a holiday camp for inmates but is thinking of a prison system that dissuades inmates from re-offending once they are released from jail.

Tip: Identify the misrepresentation and bring the discussion back to the original point. For example, 'I agree with you that there are more important things than convenience but the reasons why I do not support conscription are
a................b..................c...................'

Argumentum ad numerum

Safety in numbers

Examples

'Sixty million French people can't be wrong'

'Thousands of people read their horoscopes everyday; there must be something in it.'

It can be very reassuring to know that one's views are shared or supported by others. It is even more tempting to believe that those views are true when millions hold those same views. History shows us that often people of one generation no longer share the commonly accepted views of an earlier generation. Even if these views were accepted as true by millions. It seems ridiculous now that our predecessors thought the earth flat or that there were such things as goblins and angels. Yet this was accepted by nearly all. Beware though, what is readily accepted today could also be thought daft in the future.

Tip: Divorce the number of people who support the argument from the argument itself and examine the ideas or issues that remain, before making your decision. Remember the majority view could be correct!

Red Herring

This fallacy originates from when the fox hunting community used certain fish to discover which hounds would not be diverted by a false trail.

Examples

'You say there are people in Africa starving but what about people in this country, there are a lot of down and outs without housing, you know.'

'Coal miners want a 35 hour working week and yet in Bolivia the coal miners work an 80 hour week.'

'You say this government is making a fine mess of things, but if you think back you'll remember the last government didn't do any better.'

As you can see the subject matter at hand is changed, either deliberately or innocently and the original point is lost.

Tip: If someone is changing the subject or introducing a Red Herring one has to say, in the case of the coal miners, 'yes, you may be right about the miners in Bolivia but I really want to focus on the issue at hand.' Then, return to the original argument.

The Moderate View

This type of ploy is most regularly used in the field of politics. The proponent is attempting to undermine opposition parties and give credibility to his own party.

'If you vote socialist you will get loony lefties in and if you vote conservative you will end up with a load of reactionaries. So why not choose the Liberal Democrats, they have moderate policies.'

By painting opponents as extreme on both sides of the political spectrum the speaker can then adopt a central position which they will portray as moderate, safe, or the option of fair compromise.

What is wrong with this view?

Let us step outside of politics and consider some other examples. In the world of mathematics we can apply the same reasoning techniques, hopefully to demonstrate the absurdity of this position. For argument's sake pretend you are not familiar with square root calculations and you need to know the square root of 81. You ask 3 friends.

A says – the square root of 81 is 9
B says – nonsense the square root of 81 is 11
C says – Both wrong the square root of 81 is 13

If we follow the reasoning technique of the moderate, then B's answer would be the correct one. The answers provided by both A and C are extreme and if you aren't sure about the calculations choose the centre view, it's safest!

To illustrate the absurdity further we will consider another example. This time a head of a security firm requires a new employee to protect a retail warehouse that has suffered a spate of break-ins of late. They interview three prospective candidates for the job.

Candidate A – Has a criminal record of Burglary & Theft, 27 convictions over 25 years.

Candidate B – Has a criminal record of 14 incidents of robbery.
Candidate C – Has no criminal record whatsoever

It is fairly obvious that the security firm should choose B and avoid the extremes of both A and C! At least according to the view for moderation.

When we are faced with a range of options one should choose the option that is true or most likely to be true. Considerations of a central ground can be irrelevant or misleading. Try to judge situations on their merits.

Truth by Consensus

Examples

'Everyone agrees it must be true.'

'Truth is what we make it.'

This fallacy is similar to the fallacy *Argumentum ad numerum*.

However the implication here is that 'reality' is of our choosing and not something independent of humans. Further, the 'truth' can change over time, if we so wish it.

This is a somewhat strange view but how could we disprove it?

Let us assume that the truth is what we decide. We discuss this matter thoroughly and come to the consensus view that the truth is not what we decide but it has independence for us to try and discover!

If 'truth by consensus' is to be followed what would one make of the following position? Friends discussing the problems of congested traffic concluded that it was everybody else's responsibility to use public transport more and drive less!

The problem with the view 'that the truth is what we make it' is that it allows the possibility of a contradictory state of affairs. Further, we are left with no method for choosing which alternative is the better.

> *It is a capital mistake to theorise before one has data. Insensibly one begins to twist facts to suit theories, instead of theories to suit facts.*

PART THREE
Fallacies of Ambiguity

Often these fallacies occur when clarity and/or consistency is compromised. This is easily done but once again it could be deliberate and not just an oversight. Whichever is the case, the conclusion, whether true or false, is said to be unsupported. With these fallacies we must watch for words or terms that change their meaning during the course of an argument. Also, we need be wary of sentences that convey more than one meaning.

'Economical with the Truth'

This notorious expression came to light during a 'spy trial', when a member of the UK civil service admitted under cross examination that he had been 'economic with the truth'. He maintained that he had not lied but it transpired that he had also not been forthcoming with the entire truth of the matter. If one watched the comedy 'Yes Minister' based on life in the civil service, one would have witnessed such acts of intrigue and deceit as commonplace. Unfortunately such actions are not just confined to comedy sketches, but are regular features of political life. Withholding the truth from public inspection is not a formal fallacy but is a form of intellectual dishonesty that cannot be accepted in logical thinking.

One of the ambitions of logic is to provide the means that allows us to arrive at conclusions, which are true. Arriving at the truth is no easy matter, as any reader of philosophy will tell you. Withholding information and deceiving people will only frustrate this ambition. It may be tempting in some situations to withhold information in order to 'win the argument', however if one wishes to achieve the benefits of logical thinking such intellectual dishonesty must be proscribed.

The use and abuse of statistics

It is of the highest importance in the art of detection to be able to recognise out of a number of facts which are incidental and which vital. Otherwise your energy and attention must be dissipated instead of being concentrated.

Why should logical thinkers be wary about the use of statistics? Consider the possible following newspaper headline

'White-collar workers, more honest than blue-collar workers'

The newspaper went on to report that a survey had shown that blue-collar workers only declared 40% of their income whereas white-collar workers declared 60% of theirs. Conclusion, blue-collar workers are more dishonest. True? Consider the next headline.

'Greedy white-collar workers, take £60 billion out of the economy'

PART THREE - Fallacies of Ambiguity

The magazine drawing from the same survey as the previous newspaper example went on to say that white-collar workers cost the chancellor of the exchequer £60 billion in unpaid taxes whereas blue-collar workers cost the chancellor less, £40 billion. Conclusion: 'white-collar workers are more dishonest'?
True?

Both the magazine and the newspaper focused on different aspects of the same set of statistics, producing contrary conclusions. To understand this manipulation, one has to unpack the statistics. The key factors that gave the apparent contradiction were as follows.

a) The white-collar workers had much higher salaries on average than the blue-collar workers.

b) In a survey like this example it is impossible to ask the entire population so a sample has to be made. The sample can be all-important because the final figures will reflect the proportion of white-collar workers to blue-collar workers included in the survey.

The newspaper, for whatever reason, had found it necessary to emphasise the percentage difference between the two groups where as the magazine had focused upon the total amounts.

Was either conclusion correct?
In situations like this it does seem difficult to feel confident about a satisfactory conclusion. There are further worries also about such surveys, how do we know if people questioned told the truth and might one group be more coy about confessing to tax evasions than the other group?

39

A literal application of statistical information can lead to absurd results. Consider the following. 'Most of us have an above average number of legs.' This is because there are some people who are unfortunate to have one or no legs and three legged people are very rare!

Amphiboly

Examples

'Early this morning I paid the milkman dressed only in my nightgown'

'A policeman who lived on the opposite side of the valley to the members of his local Watch Committee, reported that some strange things had been happening in the woods between them.'

Or a recent suggestion in the local newspaper-

'Recycle cardboard and waste paper'

One has to be careful when putting forward arguments. The premises contained must not be as ambiguous as the statements in the examples above. One could present a perfectly valid argument, only to have it lose its impact by sloppy terminology.

Tip: remember that clarity is a pre-requisite of logical thinking.

Accent

Be careful this is a slippery one designed to portray the wrong impression. Emphasis is used to suggest a meaning different from the actual content of the proposition.

Example

Two executives are rivals for the same promotion. One says of the other, 'Brown hasn't touched drugs this week.'

Take note that Brown's competitor for the job has probably not said anything that is untrue. Brown hasn't taken drugs. However, the nature of the sentence suggests that Brown has taken drugs in previous weeks. When confronted with such a situation it is simply best to ask for a clarification from the person making the statement.

'Does Brown normally take drugs then?'

Tip: Ask the person making the remark for clarification and not Brown himself.

Accent is commonly used in advertising to mislead the gullible public.

Example 1

90% Fat Free!

Often used to deceive the health conscious public. There still remains 10% fat that could be a rather high percentage.

Example 2

50% OFF
On limited lines only

The advertiser is creating the impression of bargains to be had but once inside the shop one finds only a small selection of items reduced by half.

Fallacy of composition

Examples

'A car uses fewer petrochemicals and causes less pollution than a bus. Therefore cars are less environmentally damaging than buses.'

'Each player has remarkable individual talent. We should therefore expect to see a great team in action.'

The nature of this fallacy is that what is true of the parts is not necessarily true of the whole. The team players may have great individual talent but if they lacked, for example, the right tactics or teamwork they might fail. So nothing is guaranteed.

Tip: In the case of the polluting cars and buses it is true that an individual bus produces more pollution than an individual car. You have to show that the car is only part of the transport system and that if one takes the whole view then many cars conveying people produce more pollution than one bus conveying many people.

Fallacy of Division

Opposite to the fallacy of composition

Examples

'That team that won the world cup was brilliant. She played in that team so she must have been brilliant.'

PART THREE - Fallacies of Ambiguity

'Because we have survival instincts it is clear that each gene in our body is designed to survive and manipulate for its own purposes.'

'America's a wealthy country, all the people there must enjoy a good standard of living.'

'Iran is a religious country, thus each Iranian is a religious person.'

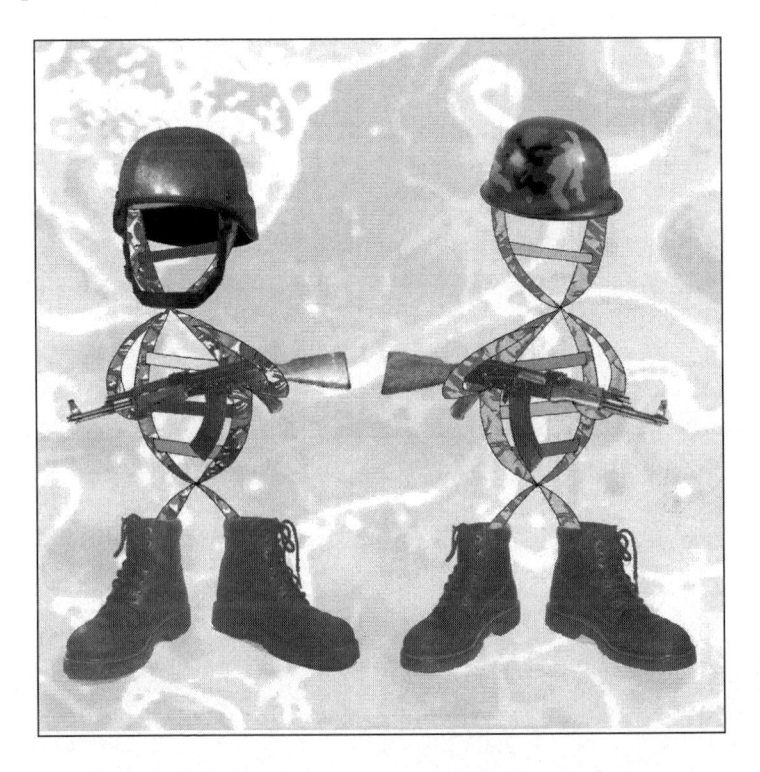

Figure 1. Because we have survival instincts it is clear that each gene in our body is designed to survive and manipulate for its own purposes.

When one sees news items or documentaries on Iran one often sees religious leaders in their parliament and women dressed from head to toe in the chador. This form of dress in public is a legal requirement of the Islamic state. It does not follow that all women conforming to this dress code are religious. There are many secular thinkers in Iran who oppose theocracy and seek a non-religious state.

Equally one may think that all Israelis hate Palestinians and yet there are a number of Israeli groups who are willing to stand in front of their own countrymen's guns, as a brave peace gesture, to protect threatened Palestinians.

What is true of the whole may not be true of the parts. In the other example the team may have been brilliant overall but the female player could have had a bad or indifferent performance during the tournament. Coaches sometimes like to maintain the same team even if one player is under performing.

Tip: One may have to describe why the parts are different and not the same as the whole. Give a simple example to demonstrate how absurd such an argument could be:

'Grass is green therefore the atoms that comprise it are green'.

It has long been an axiom of mine that the little things are infinitely the most important.

Fallacy of four terms/Equivocation

Examples

'I wanted to be a child psychologist.'
Don't be silly it takes years of training to become a Psychologist. It's not something children can do.

'All banks are beside rivers; you will therefore find Barclays banks dotted along the River Thames.'

'Everyone should fight for their beliefs. So if you disagree with me I will punch you on the nose.'

'A law implies a lawgiver. Now the Universe is full of laws – the law of gravitation and many others, hence it follows that the Universe has a lawgiver.'

This error is often subtle and difficult to detect. It is where a

47

The Red Herring and the Power of Logic

term is used to mean one thing in an argument and then another meaning later in the argument. In the case of the lawgiver, the ambiguous term refers to the types of laws that exist. On the one hand there are laws, which we humans construct through government and the judiciary, which are 'prescriptive laws' On the other hand are the laws, which we detect in nature, which are 'descriptive laws'. These latter laws are our recognition of uniform patterns that occur in nature and would exist regardless of our perceptions. Whereas the laws that are the foundation of our legal system are purely of our own construction. In the example of the lawgiver the user slips innocently from our sense of law to the other.

Tip: Identify the word that is used twice or ambiguously and demonstrate that the word is appropriate in one context but not in the other.

The more bizarre a thing is the less mysterious it proves to be. It is your commonplace, featureless fallacies (crimes) which are really puzzling, just as a commonplace face is the most difficult to identify

PART FOUR
Fallacies of Definition

Achieving the correct definition for an item under discussion or consideration is not always that easy. Too many fallacies are committed when the definition, on the one hand is too broad and includes parts that should not be included. And on the other hand when the definition is too narrow and excludes parts that should be included. We must also be watchful for definitions that are vague, self contradictory or circular. By circular, we mean that the term being defined is part of the definition itself.

The Natural Law Fallacy/Appeal to Nature

Examples

'You never see animals of the same sex trying to mate, that shows that homosexuality is unnatural.'

'In the Stone Age, males would form a group and expedite hunting missions in the search for food. Nowadays it is only natural for the man to go out to work and be the provider whilst women stay at home and care for the children.'

'I only eat organic foods, they are more natural.'

An appeal to nature or to natural products is often a convincing way to get your message across or sell your product. Sometimes it is true that what derives from nature is good for you but be aware there are also lots of things in nature that are harmful. Lots of plants, although natural, can be poisonous. Unstable naturally occurring elements such as uranium emit radiation and exposure to such is harmful to humans.

Being natural doesn't guarantee that it is in our interests. In the example of the Stone Age lifestyle our ancestors did many things which most of us would probably not consider desirable today. How many of us would wish to live in a cave, for example. Our ancestors suffered many privations and accordingly their life expectancy was much lower that the one we enjoy today. We have evolved and our changed behaviour is more adapted to our new environment, what suited us in the past may not suit us today. Homosexuality is thought by some to be unnatural and yet many other species practise this.

Tip: Organic food may be good to use, not because it is labelled natural, but because it is supposed to be free from pesticides or fertilizers that could degrade the soil. Judge things on their merits.

One's ideas must be as broad as Nature if they are to interpret Nature.

"No True Scotsman"

Examples

Ali – 'All Muslims go regularly to the mosque.'
Sally – 'Really, I know several Muslims who rarely go to the mosque.'
Ali – 'but are they "real" Muslims?'

'No Scotsman puts sugar on his porridge'
'Angus does'
'Angus is not a true Scotsman'

'Which cricket team do you support when England play the West Indies?'
If you support the West Indies then you are no true Englishman.'

'There is no such thing as a 'New Man.' All men, however they try, retain a degree of chauvinism.'

When we look at the case of the Scotsman, the arguer in what is called an 'ad hoc' fashion changes the definition. In other words he has changed the definition to support his assertion. Sometimes the criteria for a quality, such as achieving a New Man status, is set so high and severe that it is doubtful that any person could live to the ideal set.

One does hear from time to time of such statements as, 'she's not truly English, she holidays in France' or 'how can he be a socialist he owns private property.' It is rare that people live fully to an ideal however hard they aspire to it.

Tip: Reducing the argument to symbols one can see that the 'No True Scotsman' move ensures that a claim is true simply by definition.

e.g.	All A's are B's
	X is an A but X is not a B
	Therefore X is not a true A
	(because only A's that are B's are true A's)

The Extended Analogy

Examples

'If you want to be successful in life think of how you would approach a game of monopoly. You build up capital, invest in property, take a few chances but don't be too ambitious and the returns will come in.'

'If you want to know the true politics of the Green Party think of a water melon – green on the outside but red through the middle.'

Analogy can be a useful tool when explaining unfamiliar ideas with the use of something more familiar as an illustration. However, be aware, that analogies, which are not totally accurate in their portrayal, can be used unfairly to undermine an argument.

In the example of the watermelon, the speaker is trying to discredit the Green party by suggesting, with the powerful psychological picture, that their politics are either socialist or communist. The analogy is inaccurate because although the Green Party may hold some policies that could be described as having a socialist leaning, it is however a mistake to suggest that they are overwhelmingly red.

Tip: Try to think if the picture presented in an analogy really does match the reality. Quite often when one examines analogies in detail differences start to appear and the analogy breaks down.

Monopoly is not like real life at all. In the game all the contestants start off on an equal footing, which is hardly the case in reality. Further, when you come into life, unlike the game, someone already owns the property and has devised rules (laws) to protect it. So the analogy is inadequate.

Begging the Question

A variation of arguments that are circular.
Fallacy of interrogation or presupposition

Examples

'Have you stopped beating your husband?'

'Are there any times when you don't think about sex?'

'After you robbed the bank which car did you use for a getaway?'

You are probably familiar with these types of questions, they are heavily loaded so one has to be careful how one replies. Sometimes they add an extra barb: 'Are there any times when you don't think about sex, answer yes or no?'

If you give a yes or no answer then either way you commit yourself to the admission that you often think about sex. The 'answer yes or no' is an illegitimate move, but if you say that you can't give a yes/no answer it could look as if you are trying to avoid the question.

Tip: Difficult. Rather than answer the question, point out that it takes the form of begging the question or is loaded against your answer.

Reification/Hypostatization

Examples

'I doubt if there is such a thing as evolution, no one can see it, hear it, touch it, or taste it, so what is it?'

'Mary lost her temper yesterday'
'Oh dear, if you tell me what it looks like I will try to find it for her.'

This is not a common fallacy and the example concerning Mary and her temper was not one drawn from real life but purely as an illustration of what happens when someone confuses an abstract concept as a material thing.

Answers that are not Answers

Have you ever sat around in a group discussing the mysteries of life when someone contributes the 'wisest' of insights, 'well whatever happens, was meant to happen'? They then sit back satisfied and unchallenged having delivered a pearl of ancient wisdom.

PART FOUR - Fallacies of Definition

However seductive this may sound on first impression, closer examination shows that nothing has been said that illuminates any mystery.

Because of the statement's tautological nature, it can never be proved wrong. If event A happens it was meant to, if event B happens it also was meant to, the same for events C, D, E, F.... In fact any event that happens was meant to. So what use is this insight?

In fact it is of no value whatsoever because it has no predictive power concerning future events and also it explains nothing. It gives no explanation as to why events occurred and no clue to possible future events.

Another popular example of this type of wisdom occurs when discussing such issues as the origins of the universe or the origins of life. Let us as an example look at the origin of the universe argument. Someone of a scientific mind may argue that because the universe is expanding in a uniform manner from a central area, it is not unreasonable to suggest that it all began with condensed matter and the 'big bang'. The conversation continues and some people are not satisfied with this explanation and ask the pertinent question, 'but what happened prior to the big bang and what caused it?' At this point the proponent of the big bang admits that she is at a loss to explain this and doubt is thrown over the theory. But then she asks the doubters how they think the universe began.

Often the 'answer' returned can be 'I think God created the universe'. But is this an answer?

For now the scientifically minded woman asks, 'did God

begin the universe with a big bang, or if not, then by what means?'

Now, it may be the case that God created the universe but the answer to the question concerning the universe origins has not been answered. The supposed answer is not an answer at all but the introduction of another mystery. We now have the new mystery of whether God created the universe and the mystery of the mechanics which God employed.

It is at this point that philosophers invoke what is known as Ockham's razor named after William Ockham (1285 - 1347), an English Franciscan. His methodological device argued for simplicity over complexity, where complexity offers nothing of any extra value. One should not multiply mysteries unnecessarily; the razor is employed to sever any unhelpful appendages.

The same procedure also applies to the mystery of how organic life arose from the inorganic; invoking supernatural explanations for the transition creates unnecessary complexity and should also therefore succumb to Ockham's razor. Intellectual honesty in logical reasoning allows us to admit that we do not have all the solutions to life's mysteries. There is nothing wrong with saying, 'I just don't know!' This is more honest approach than inventing unsatisfactory solutions to ease any uncomfortable feelings of uncertainty.

Everything becomes nothing

People in conversation or in written works can get over ambitious and make claims for the all-pervading existence of certain qualities. Unfortunately insistence on this pervading existence may undermine the quality they are promoting.

To make this clearer let us consider an example from a Jerome K Jerome novel, "Tommy & Co." An argument is put forward claiming that all humans are selfish. There are no exceptions and no one is capable of altruistic behaviour. To justify this claim the person in the novel recognises that people do perform actions that on the surface look altruistic, because one person is seen to help another. However, the motivation for this apparent altruistic behaviour is for a satisfying self-fulfilment or pleasure. According to this view, everyone who performs an action like helping an old man cross the road or rescuing someone in danger will get a feeling of pleasure. Subsequently all our actions are based upon satisfying our desire for these pleasures. No one is altruistic, it is a myth, and everyone is selfish, the argument concludes.

Well, let us assume that the argument is true for the time being and that all our actions are selfish. If we rob a bank it is a selfish act, if we give money to Oxfam it is also a selfish act. According to the theory both acts are pursued to gain personal satisfaction. In fact every act we performed in the past and every act that we will perform in the future will be a selfish act also. Now because every act is included, there will certainly be some selfish acts that will help others also and some selfish acts that only benefit the individual. If I perform the selfish act of giving blood I may benefit other people. If I put a brick through my neighbour's car windscreen I am performing a selfish act but almost certainly not benefiting anyone.

There are then different types of selfish acts, those that might benefit others and those that might benefit only the individual. So one could say that some selfish acts are good and some bad or, in the least, that some selfish acts are better than other selfish acts.

We are now in a position to evaluate selfish acts and decide which acts we might think we ought or ought not to carry out. The important question arises, is there any point in calling these different acts selfish? Surely what really matters is whether the acts are considered good or bad, right or wrong. The description of the acts as selfish does nothing to help our judgement as to whether we should perform X or Y. Describing all acts as selfish can therefore be discarded. The use of the description selfish becomes valueless when considered in this light. Normally we think of a selfish act as one where we think of ourselves only and do not take others into consideration, but Jerome's character in the book extends and universalises the idea of selfish behaviour. The consequence of this is that it becomes meaningless because there is no longer any contrast between selfish and unselfish behaviour.

This type of universalisation has manifested itself recently in a religious context. The decline in faith in the west has led people to question the concept of God as a monolithic force, or as a single figurehead. Instead we hear the belief that God is all around, all pervasive. God is all things. This is not a new idea but a revival from Benedictus Spinoza (1632 - 1677) who said that all things are in God and everything takes place by the laws alone of the infinite nature of God.

This view no longer sees God as an anthropomorphic figure, conducting events from outside the universe, but now God is

PART FOUR - Fallacies of Definition

seen as the same thing as nature. Can we make sense of this view? If God is all things, then not only the tangible objects that we see every day are a manifestation of God in some way, but also the sub atomic particles, which can't be seen are said also to be God.

God becomes everything and every thing becomes God.

The logical outcome of Spinoza's view does seem to make God rather redundant. God no longer has any special qualities that would separate God from nature. They are one and the same. I would argue that if one is to believe in God then God must be given distinctive qualities otherwise the fallacy of 'everything becomes nothing' is committed.

59

PART FIVE
Causal and Faulty Inductive Fallacies

A common mistake is to simply get the causes of an event or series of events wrong. Connections are made where none should be made. Usually this is done innocently when the full facts of the case are not laid bare and hasty generalizations follow. However, it is also sometimes the case that unscrupulous individuals withhold information or construct false analogies that could pervert final conclusions.

Cum hoc ergo propter hoc

'With this, therefore because of this.' Mistaken causes

Examples

'More young women are smoking and drinking to excess than ever before. This is the consequences of Feminism'.

'Crime rates have risen whilst church attendances have fallen. We need to get people back to church before this country becomes morally bankrupt.'

This fallacy is committed when two events occur at the same time and where one is thought to cause the other. Crime rates for example can be influenced by lots of factors. If the Police employ more policemen in a certain area and they are successful in detecting crime, then the crime rate automatically goes higher. The statement also implies that morality is the province of the church exclusively, yet we probably receive our morals from a multitude of sources, i.e. family, friends, school or media.

Tip: Search for all the factors that influence events. One is quite entitled to doubt causal explanations if the 'causal mechanisms' are dubious or obscure. For example, we can often see why a medicine cures an illness but it is difficult to see why a magic charm might produce the same effect. Beware, sometimes people are looking to undermine a particular creed or body of opinion and wrongly attribute unfavourable consequences that are not necessarily related to those beliefs. This fallacy is sometimes referred to as the 'Correlation Fallacy'.

Examples

'If I wash my car it rains'

'In the past very few people could read and write, there was very little graffiti. Now that everyone can read and write there is graffiti everywhere.'

Because different events have occurred at the same time it is tempting to ascribe some form of casual relationship, when really the events are quite independent of each other.

These are obvious examples of fallacy but one has to be careful because often they can be much more subtle, and seductive. Especially if the person targeted already wishes to believe in the alleged benefits of the casual relationship.

Tip: Wash your car after it stops raining.

Post hoc ergo propter hoc

'After this therefore because of this'

Examples

'We (the new government) have only been in office three months and already the economy is booming.'

'I tried the Indian rain dance three times now and afterwards it has always rained. That proves there is something in it.'

Politicians are often keen to take credit even if it's through no effort of their own. The economy booming was unlikely to be caused by the introduction of a new government. Economic performances are the product of more long-term policies but it is often difficult to pinpoint the exact causes.

Tip: Ask yourself – coincidence or cause?

Just imagine what may happen if everyone in the world were to practise rain dancing, we would have non-stop rain! In this

Non sequitur

'it does not follow'

Examples

'I own a fast sports car, women love me.'

'Cover your body otherwise you won't go to heaven'

'Wear what you like, God is forgiving.'

Or as attempted in humour-

'I have good experience with children, I used to be one.'

Broadly speaking the conclusion cannot be supported by the premises as it does not follow. Non sequiturs are often used in humour but they are still fallacies.

Non causa pro causa

The false cause fallacy

Examples

'I prayed all week that our hockey players might win the match on Saturday. Sure enough we did, so that proved that God was listening.'

'I had been feeling so tired and lethargic recently so I decided to visit an alternative therapist. She rubbed a spring onion all over me, releasing its spiritual essence into my body. Now I feel great.'

People often attribute the wrong cause to explain an event. The hockey team probably won because of alternative reasons such as better teamwork, taken opportunities, more training etc. Also remember that is was equally possible that supporters of the opposing team could also have prayed to God for their team to win.

In the case of the alternative therapist it could be argued that the person felt better because they believed they would benefit from the treatment. In medicine this is known as the placebo effect. When testing new drugs researchers include a sample of sugar pills (placebos) that are taken by unsuspecting volunteers or patients. It is surprising how often people who are unwittingly taking these sugar pills report beneficial results.

Tip: Think of alternative causes when presented with such an argument. In the case of the spring onion, ask what these spiritual properties actually are? Do other vegetables possess them? How do the practitioners come to know about these 'remarkable' but doubtful properties?

'The exception proves the rule'

When I was younger I always felt uncomfortable whenever this expression was used. Later in life I discovered what was exactly wrong with it.

The expression actually runs contrary to logic, philosophical thinking and scientific methodology. It states that if you find an exception to the rule, or something that gives cause to doubt the rule, then the rule is proved to be okay or strengthened. As you can guess this is nonsense!

If a scientist said for example, we will be able to witness a particular comet every 7 years. We then discovered that on the second time of seeing the comet the gap between sightings was only 6 years. If the astronomer then said yes my prediction is still okay, it is the exception that confirms my theory, then we would think them crazy. And rightly so.

Take another example

Speaker A) We never get any Asians elected as MPs.
Speaker B) Yes we did. Last year Ali Akbar was elected in Bradford.
Speaker A) Well that exception proves my original point. (the rule)

Sheer nonsense and yet this argument is commonly used. What's gone wrong?

When the expression was originally used in past centuries it had a different meaning. The word 'prove' in those times also meant – 'test', so this expression can be reworded as this – 'it is the exception that tests the rule'.

As I see it, the original meaning is what we should accept, an exception 'tests' or challenges a rule and does not confirm it. Some may be familiar with the old saying 'the proof of the pudding is in the eating.' This is representative of the original meaning of 'proof.'

> *I never make exceptions. An exception disproves the rule*

If a scientist who was conducting an experiment to test a hypothesis, discovered that some of the results ran contrary to her expectations then she would check her data, check her experiment was functioning correctly and check that all the necessary steps in the experiment were achieved correctly. She does this because the results she has recorded have challenged the confirmation she seeks. If she repeats the experiment and still gets exceptions in her evidence it is very likely that she would abandon the hypothesis.

Dicto simpliciter

Sweeping Generalizations

Examples

'Protestants don't normally marry Catholics. You are a Protestant therefore you should not marry a Catholic.'

'Palestinians and Israelis don't get on together. You are Jewish therefore you don't like Palestinians.'

'Girls do better than boys in exams. I therefore expect my daughter to perform better than all the boys in her class.'

'Our ancestors were forced to hunt for their food to survive. Hunting is therefore natural to our behaviour because we have inherited our ancestors' genes.'

This is the case where a general rule is extended to cover all situations. It may be the case that Palestinians and Jews don't generally get on but this doesn't stop individual friendships occurring.

There may have been a need for our ancestors to hunt but because we have evolved over thousands of years our nature may have changed. Our disposition to hunt (if we had such) may have been replaced by other forms of behaviour.

Tip: Be careful when you go from the general rule to a specific situation. Or what you can say of most is not necessarily what you can say of all.

Bifurcation

False Dilemma or the Black and White argument

Examples

"Either you're with me or against me."

'If we don't embark upon a major road building programme then the existing roads will soon become completely choked up.'

'Either you favour spending more money on defence or you favour allowing other nations to dictate our foreign policy.'

These types of arguments are presented as if there are only two solutions, yet really there are other options available. In the case of the road-building programme it is easy to see that there are other alternatives, such as increased spending on public transport or more taxes and restrictions on car use.

Tip: Ask yourself if there is really a limited number of options or if there is a middle way or further alternatives available to be considered.

Anecdotal evidence

Examples

'Old Bill, the ironmonger, smoked a packet of cigarettes every day of his life and he went on until he was 98 before he passed away. That proves that smoking is not bad for you.'

'Criminals should complete their full term penalty. Only the other day they let out that rapist early and within a month he had assaulted another victim.'

'I read in my Stars Horoscope that I was going to be lucky and sure enough I won £50 from the lottery on the same day. There has to be something in Astrology.'

Anecdotal evidence can be very persuasive, especially when the intended audience want to believe the main points in an argument. It is a favourite ploy of politicians, religious preachers and TV interviewers. The trick is to find a selective instance that undermines or re-enforces an argument. Old Bill may have smoked a packet of cigarettes a day but no one is saying that every single person that smokes will die early of cancer, but that the chances of contracting cancer are much higher if one smokes.

Tip: Ask yourself if the anecdote is representative? Does every criminal let out early re-offend? Is the evidence of the lucky lottery ticket sufficient for faith in horoscopes?

Argumentum ad opus est.

Appeal to hard work

Examples

'The Devil finds work for idle hands.'

'When Choke a cola opens a new plant in Africa, they bring jobs to the local population.'

'Saudi Arabia signed a contract with a security firm from England. The Ministry of Defence spokesperson said this would secure employment for the locals for the next two years.'

Although providing employment can be beneficial for individuals or the community as a whole it is absurd to think that this is always the case. If it were always the case one could say 'thanks heavens for criminals, if there were no criminals the police would be out of work.'

Or even

'It's a good thing that 'AIDS' exists, think of all the hospital staff that depend upon that and other diseases for their livelihoods.'

Tip: Some forms of work we could do without, so does the work-generating scheme provide anything beneficial?

Circulus in demonstrando

Circular Argument also known as *Petitio Principii*

Examples

'Everything that happens is meant to happen.'

'It says in the Bible that God exists. Since the Bible is God's word and God never speaks falsely, then everything in the Bible must be true, so God must exist.'

'Paranormal phenomena exist because I have had experiences that can only be described as paranormal.'

'You should vote in elections because if you don't you will undermine our democracy. Then you won't be able to vote for anyone.'

These types of argument are very widespread. They commit the sin of reproducing the original premise in the conclusion, hence the circularity. Take the argument of the Fatalist, 'everything that happens is meant to happen', this is impossible to disprove but because of its tautological nature it tells us absolutely nothing. People who declare it often act as if there is something profound and illuminating that has been discovered, but the statement is of no value.

Tip: When you are putting forward an argument try to justify it without simply repeating the premise in conclusion. In the example of supporting voting at elections, you should add something similar to-

'if you don't vote at elections then democracy will collapse and it is possible that either law and order could break down or at the other extreme a dictatorship be established.

Hasty Generalization/Converse Accident

Examples

'Johnathan Archer was a corrupt politician. Therefore all politicians are corrupt.'

'I know that rock bands smoke dope, only the other day I read in the Daily Observer that the police busted the Rolling Stones.'

'I asked several friends at the Rotary club who they are voting for in the forthcoming election, they all said Conservative. So it looks like they will form the next government.'

'We went to Spain and had our car broken into twice within a fortnight. You can't trust the Spanish.'

Another common error that one often hears in every day conversation. The generalization is hasty because it is based on a selective instance rather then deep experience or a structured study.

It's always good to check the conclusions of opinion pollsters. How large was their sample? Was it a fair representation of views?

Tip: one can give counter examples to demonstrate the fallacious arguments. In the case of travelling to Spain one could say that I know of friends that visit Spain regularly and they have never been robbed. (Providing that is the case of course.)

> *I never guess. It is a shocking habit - destructive to the logical faculty.*

Slippery Slopes

Examples

'If we legalize pot, then it will only be a matter of time before the users move on to harder drugs such as heroin.'

'If we continue to allow abortions to be practised it will only be a matter of time before infanticide is condoned.'

'I'm sorry I can't give you pay rise, if I do the others will find out about it and they will want a pay rise too. The company just can't afford the extra expenditure.'

This fallacy takes the form of the following example.

If x occurs then it will cause y
y will in turn cause z
z is undesirable
Therefore we should not do x

The fallacy occurs when there is no connection between the postulated harmful effects and the original idea. The person employing the slippery slope argument must show that the actions under consideration will lead without exception to undesirable results. In some instances when the slippery slope argument is deployed, not everyone views the consequences that may follow as harmful. For example in the 19th century it was argued by some that votes for working men, if accepted, could lead to votes for women!

Tip: Try to establish if there is a necessary or causal connection and if the likely consequences are harmful or beneficial. The statement, 'if we legalize pot, then it will only be a matter of time before the users move on to harder drugs such as heroin,' would be better if it was re-written to something like the following. 'There is some evidence to suggest that if we legalize pot, then it will only be a matter of time before some of the users move on to harder drugs such as heroin.'

We now turn to formal logic and examine how Logicians construct arguments. We begin with the basic building blocks of logic- premises.

PART SIX
Formal Logic

What is a premise?

A premise could be a fact, a piece of data or any statement used as a starting point in an argument. The statement could be true, false or assumed. Further, it is a type of statement that you can connect together with another statement, just as you would connect pieces of a jigsaw puzzle.

Once you have connected your premises together correctly you can arrive at a conclusion. Similarly with the puzzle, once the pieces are interlocked properly one can see a picture.

In logic you don't always have the benefit that the jigsaw puzzler has of a picture, to guide you. You may have an idea of the final picture but until the pieces are connected you do not know if the picture is correct. (When you piece premises together you may arrive at a picture that was not expected.)

Example

Premise A The murderer is one of the following, Ms Scarlet, Colonel Mustard, Professor Moriarty or Doctor Black.

Premise B The Police have correctly eliminated – 'Colonel Mustard, Professor Moriarty and Doctor Black.'

Conclusion Ms Scarlet was the offender

A B = CONCLUSION

Getting The Correct Premises

A premise could be true or false. Sometimes we have the wrong piece of information and if we piece it together with another piece we get the wrong picture or a false conclusion.

Premise A   Barry is a boy
Premise B   All four-year-old boys smoke cigars
Conclusion   Barry smokes cigars

Premise B is not a correct fact about the world, as we know it. Most of us have never heard of any four year olds smoking, let alone all four years olds.

> TRUE PREMISE
> +
> FALSE PREMISE
> =
> FALSE CONCLUSION

(Careful. Although the conclusion is false the argument could still be valid! See section on validity below)

What happens in real life?

Someone may come along and say that Barry smokes cigars. You think this is a little odd so you ask the person, what makes him think that? They answer that they saw an article in the newspaper about 4-year olds smoking. You reply that's it's a bit dubious and that they might just be making it up.

When you are unhappy about a conclusion or think it is a little fishy then go back and look at the reasons or premises to see if you think they are true.

Validity

In the last example of the four year old smoking cigars we arrived at a conclusion that was false. However in Logic although the conclusion was said to be false the reasoning was still valid. What does this mean?

If we think of our jigsaw pieces again but this time imagine they are all blank. Although they are blank we can still fit them together correctly. This is what logicians do when they link premises together in a valid form.

Example

1st Premise	All x are A
2nd Premise	p is X
Therefore	All p are A

This conclusion is said to follow from the premises therefore the argument is valid. The blank jigsaw puzzle pieces fit together correctly but we do not know if the picture is correct until we colour each piece. So if we substitute

X = All boys and A = smoke cigars
p = Barry

We can then see that the picture for the puzzle is wrong even if the pieces fit together. The argument is said to be valid (fits together by shape) but the conclusion is false. (The end picture is wrong)

Validity Can Produce Peculiar Results

Consider the following syllogism

Premise A	All females are authors	False
Premise B	Charles Dickens is female	False
Conclusion	Charles Dickens is an author	True

We must be aware that the argument is valid and the conclusion true even though both premises are blatantly false! Further, consider another example of valid reasoning that includes one false premise and a true conclusion.

Premise A	Charles Dickens is an author	True
Premise B	All authors are English	False
Conclusion	Charles Dickens is English	True

If one or more of the premises are false and the conclusion arrived at is true, then one may ask, what use is validity? We address this next.

What use is Validity?

In some ways validity is more important than other considerations in logical thinking. Valid arguments are ones that are independent of human values. Logic doesn't tell us if 'fighting' is right or wrong, it only tells us if the reasons used to supporting such an activity are validly argued.

This is particularly useful when the premises used to support an argument are controversial. Not everyone agrees what the facts are. If there is a disagreement over the facts then we need a method to resolve this. Validity in thinking provides this.

Consider this example

Premise A	Jenny is a human
Premise B	All humans have souls
Conclusion	Jenny has a soul

This argument is valid but it is not accepted by all that we have souls. Premise B is controversial. In these circumstances we can rewrite the argument as such-

Premise A   Jenny is a human
Premise B   If all humans have souls
Conclusion   Then Jenny has a soul

See conditionals.

Validity is Truth Preserving

This is considered the 'Golden Rule ' of logic. Wherever and whenever the premises of an argument are true and the reasoning valid, then the conclusion must be true.

Example

Premise A   Charles Dickens was born before George Orwell. True
Premise B   George Orwell was born in 1903.   True
Conclusion   Charles Dickens was born before 1903. True

This is of great use, not only to mathematicians and scientists but also for everyone. Once the premises are established and we reason validly then we can build absolute firm conclusions. The great problem is often to establish the premises. If we are not certain then logic has a marvellous trick, we introduce the 'if' word. We now enter the arena of Hypothetical arguments.

The Benefits of Conditional Reasoning

Those who have played chess will be familiar with the following modes of thought-

1 If I move my Knight and threaten her Queen she has two choices.
2 If she moves her Queen then I could get checkmate.
3 If she moves her Bishop or King then I capture her Queen.
4 Either way moving my Knight will give me an advantage.
This approach is the conditional, 'if – then' approach. A chess player will run through one's own mind several 'if – then' alternatives. If I move my king then she could take my knight or if she castles then I could attack the castles, pawn etc.

The type of thought used by chess players is an important part of logical thinking. It has several advantages. For example, one can form an argument in one's mind without being committed to it. The argument becomes depersonalised and may be viewed in a more neutral light. If the premise or premises are controversial then one can construct the argument by putting the 'if '(and possibly 'only if') before the controversial premise.

These devices are necessary when in argument the passions may begin to flow, objectivity can be lost and we become blinded by trying to win the argument.

Enthymemes

An argument where the premises and/or the conclusion remain unstated.

Example

'I know someone else who didn't cooperate, the photographs were released to the press, he lost everything: his job, his wife, his career. Need I say more?"

Although not stated the person concerned is being black mailed with a threat hanging over him. The argument unfolded runs something like this:

If you don't co-operate then the photographs will be released to the press

If the photos are released then you could lose everything.

You do not want to lose everything

Therefore you had better co-operate.

This example of an enthymeme is fairly easy to unpack but often they are more subtle.

What is possible?

Another look at facts

If one said it is possible to land a manned spaced craft on Mars, it would be accepted as a statement that is true. We have sent several manned trips to the moon and if we really wanted to devote billions of pounds on a mars landing then we could achieve it if we decided to.

This is true nowadays but what would people have thought if you could have suggested a mars landing at the time of Alfred the Great. Hardly anyone then would have accepted this as a possibility. What is technically possible today was unimaginable in the past. It is also probably true that what is considered impossible today will be considered commonplace in the future.

For example, if someone said it is possible to get from Sydney to Paris in half an hour, people would laugh and doubt this.

We can draw a distinction here between what is technically possible and what is logically possible. It is technically impossible at the moment to travel from Sydney to Paris in half an hour but it is not logically impossible. It could be, unknown to us, that a form of propulsion has been developed secretly that allows this sort of extremely fast travel. Indeed it is logically possible that in the future 'grass' is coloured red, or that all humans have two heads. It could even be the case that humans live together in peace without war and strife. All of these unlikely events are logically possible. (It should be noted here that anything that is technically possible is also logically possible)

> *How often have I said to you that when you have eliminated the impossible, whatever remains, however improbable, must be the truth?*

One may ask oneself at this junction just what sort of things can be both technically and logically impossible? And what determines what is and what isn't logically impossible?

Logical Impossibilities

The foundations of logic are said to be tautological in nature. This means that they must be true and to deny them would involve a contradiction. These following propositions are all examples of tautologies. The opposite of each of these would be a logical impossibility.

All As are A
All widows are female
All squares have four sides

If A precedes B and B precedes C then A must precede C.

Sarah is taller than Tony and Tony is taller than Zoe then Sarah must also be taller than Zoe.

If Manchester United won the premiership exclusively in 1987 then Liverpool could not have also won it that same year.

To deny the truth of any of the above statements would be to commit a self-contradiction. One cannot say, for example, that not all As are A. Or put another way not all apples are apples. This just wouldn't make sense. 'I ate an apple but it wasn't an apple' would be a statement of sheer nonsense, a self-contradiction.

Logical statements that must be true tell us nothing about the world. For example, all black cats would be black even if there were no cats in the universe. They differ from scientific statements, which have the potential to tell us a lot about the world.

Astronomers assert that the earth orbits the sun for example. This statement could be doubted without fear of a self contradiction. As it stands all the evidence of planetary motion supports the astronomers and this is generally accepted as a true statement about the sun and the earth. However, it is still logically possible that the sun could orbit the earth. This distinction between logical possibilities and scientific possibilities is also an indication of their claims to truth.

See the truth triangle

The Truth Triangle

What counts as truth? Are some areas of our thoughts more likely to be true than others?

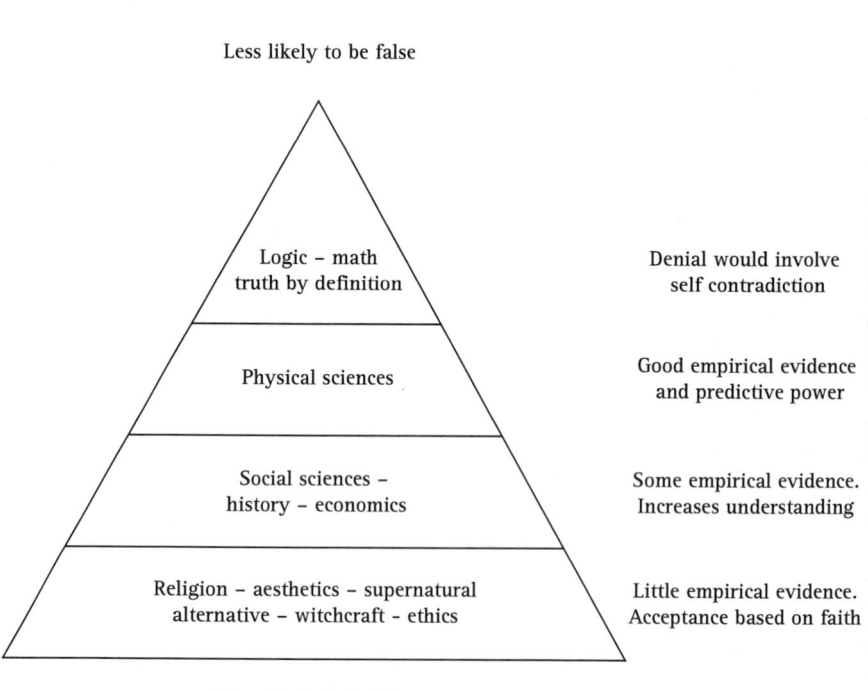

Less likely to be false

Logic – math truth by definition	Denial would involve self contradiction
Physical sciences	Good empirical evidence and predictive power
Social sciences – history – economics	Some empirical evidence. Increases understanding
Religion – aesthetics – supernatural alternative – witchcraft - ethics	Little empirical evidence. Acceptance based on faith

More likely to be false

See overleaf for an explanation of the Truth Triangle

The Truth Triangle explained.

> *It was easier to know it than to explain why I know it. If you were asked to prove that two and two made four, you might find some difficulty, and yet you are quite sure of the fact.*

Why is the category at the top of the triangle less likely to be false than the lower categories?

If one looks at the content of the top it includes such things as Logic, Maths and Truths by definition. Taking an example from maths first, let us consider the simple equation-

1 + 1 = 2

It seems that whenever and wherever we add one to one we always arrive at two. Has there ever been an occasion when we added two ones together and didn't get two? This seems always to be the case in pure mathematics and it seems highly improbable that one plus one could equal anything other than two. This position is more controversial if we step outside pure mathematics and into applied mathematics. One may be familiar with the old chestnut-

One haystack + One haystack = One haystack.

Does this cast doubt on the equation's viability? Not really, because although there is still only one haystack remaining, the weight or bio-mass has doubled. The haystack example does not confound things but consider what happens when one adds the following;

One drop of water + One drop of water = ?

We still have one drop of water but the size is not doubled! This is because the new surface tension of the resulting droplet reduces its overall size. One cannot be quite so confident with applied mathematics as one is with pure mathematics. However, to doubt pure mathematics would be considered by many to be a self-contradiction. This is termed a 'necessary truth' by philosophers. This area is still controversial with some arguing that applied mathematics falls under the category of 'necessary truths'. Nevertheless, if we contrast this with the category at the base of the triangle we can see real differences. Take religion for example, there are many religions in the world and they all hold contrary views. Some believe in Christ, some do not. Some do not have a god whereas others might worship the sun. Some believe in re-incarnation, some believe we have a soul that goes to heaven after bodily death. There is such diversity that we can deduce that they cannot all be true. (They all could be false of course.) The chances of a religion being true is low, other things being equal, one reason is because of the enormous number of diverse religions claiming to have the 'truth'. This is not the case with mathematics and logic.

We can doubt the truth of a religion but does it make sense

to doubt a principle of logic, such as all As are A? Further, as we have already mentioned, the principles of pure maths seem to hold true. Not only do they hold true at this moment in time but also they hold true for the future. One can predict that 1+1=2 will always hold true in the future. Logic and Maths have no competitors because they are tautological in their nature.

Why isn't science in the top category?

Whereas logic and maths are tautological, science and all the other categories are not. Tautologies tell us nothing about the world but science has the potential to tell us a lot. However, there is less certainty with this category because what science tells us today could be contradicted in the future. These are known as 'contingent truths.' They are called contingent because their truth is gained only from our experience. However, the history of science teaches us that science evolves over time and some of what was thought to be true in the past has changed as our understanding of the world grows. Curiously it is science that mostly furnishes its own refutations.

Why are the Physical sciences categorized above the Social Sciences and History in the truth triangle?

The social sciences contribute a lot to our understanding of the world but they do not have such a good track record when it comes to predictions. This is because the data that they work with has so many variables. They cannot be placed in a controlled environment for experimentation and subsequently we are often presented with results that are quite contrary. If one listens to a group of economists for example, they will invariably offer different prognoses for our economy. Once again they cannot all be correct. History, is often said to be written by the victorious. After a battle or war the controlling power has access to the media and print, it is their views that are reflected in the historical manuscripts. History also tends to be very nationalistic. Two different countries can have completely different accounts of the events and their causes, of any given period. Although history is valuable for understanding large-scale events it unfortunately cannot offer a very good predictive analysis.

Why aren't aesthetics, ethics and religion in a higher category?

The defining characteristics lacking in this group are that they are not tautological nor do they command much support of empirical evidence. There is a fantastic diversity of opinion, which often is prescriptive. One could find justification for almost any form of action amongst this group. It is very difficult to evaluate the merits and de-merits because the criteria are elusive.

I confess that these views are controversial. Nevertheless, it is a challenge to see how my criteria might compare with an alternative set.

Deductive or Inductive?

Two basic forms of argument employed in logic

In deductive arguments the conclusion has to be true if the premises are true and the reasoning valid.

However the conclusion of inductive arguments are not necessarily true even if the premises are true. They are said to be, however, strong or probable indicators of the truth.

Example of a deductive argument

The only green fruit in a fruit bowl are pears.
There are some apples in the bowl.
Those apples are not green.

(For further examples of deductive arguments see the section on the four basic syllogisms.)

Example of an inductive argument

Amanda doesn't like apples at all.
Amanda is eating fruit from the bowl.
In the fruit bowl there are apples, bananas and pears.
Amanda is probably eating a banana or a pear.

The first argument shows that the conclusion cannot be any other than, 'apples in the fruit bowl are not green'. However in the second argument the conclusion that Amanda is eating a banana or a pear is a reasonable one to make. However it is not necessarily true. Amanda may hate eating bananas and pears more than apples and she could be so hungry that she just has to eat something. There is nothing in the argument to proscribe this alternative conclusion or another constructed conclusion.

Science is based on 'Induction'. The type of argument we have just witnessed, the inductive argument, is a large part of the scientific method. It produces strong conclusions or theories that are highly probable but still not necessarily true. If the theories of science are only probably true why should we bother with them? Although the conclusions are not necessarily true they are still very useful and without them it would be doubtful if we could make accurate predictions.

> *Improbable as it is, all other explanations are more improbable still.*

The edge that science has over other methods or disciplines is not only its manifest success with technology, but also its close approximation with the truth. Strong inductive arguments are probably our best vehicles for understanding the world.

The Four Basic Syllogisms

These are the traditional patterns of deductive argument.

Categorical syllogisms.

Example

No socialist accepts capitalism.
Some labour party members accept capitalism.
Therefore some labour party members are not socialists.

No A are B
Some C are B
Therefore some C are not A

Disjunctive syllogisms

Example

Either Carol will arrive tonight or in the morning.
She will not arrive tonight.
Therefore Carol will arrive in the morning.

Either C or M
Not C
Therefore M

Pure Hypothetical Syllogisms

Example

If you don't save then your capital won't grow.
If your capital doesn't grow then you will not be able to spend more of the interest.
Therefore if you don't save you will not then be able to spend more of the interest.

If A then B
If B then C
Therefore if A then C

All the terms in this syllogism are conditional, if-then. This type of syllogism is fairly rare compared to the following.

Mixed hypothetical syllogisms.

(Strictly speaking these are not pure syllogisms but you will often see them described as such in many textbooks.) In modern logic however they are referred to by their Latin names: *modus ponens* and *modus tollens*.

Example of *modus ponens*

If the government introduces ID cards then our human rights will be eroded.
The government will introduce ID cards.
Therefore our human rights will be eroded.

If p is true then q is true
p is true
Therefore q is true

Example of *modus tollens*

If the government introduces ID cards then our human rights will be eroded.
Our human rights will not be eroded.
Therefore the government will not introduce ID cards.

If p is true then q is true
q is not true
Therefore p is not true

We will now consider arguments similar in form to the previous two arguments but are examples of invalid reasoning.

Affirmation of the consequent.
(a fallacious argument)

Examples

'If the universe was created by God we would see good design. We do see good design therefore the universe must have been created by God'

This type of fallacious argument takes the form, A implies B, B is true therefore A is true. Logicians use the following shorthand.

If A then B
B
Therefore A.

When an 'If...then...' statement is used, 'A' is the antecedent and 'B' is the consequent. Hence the title 'affirming the consequent.'

If you are not quite sure why the argument about God is invalid then look at he following argument, which takes the same form-

If I live in London then I live in the UK.
I do live in the UK
Therefore I live in London.

PART SIX - Formal Logic

This form of reasoning is absurd because the person could also live in, for example, Blackpool or Birmingham. It should be fairly easy to spot why the argument about God is invalid. Good design could also come about by alternative means. Most scientists would argue that the good design in nature was the product of evolution.

Be careful though. The argument may be invalid but the conclusion could still be true! In the second example the person could live in London but the argument as it stands doesn't prove it.

Tip: B may be true for other reasons. Try to think of any alternatives that may account for B.

This is a formal fallacy. See the section on the four basic syllogisms where examples of modus tollens and modus ponens demonstrate the correct forms of argument.

97

Denial of the antecedent

This argument takes the form

If A then B
Not A
Therefore, not B

Example

If I am in London I am in England.
I am not in London, therefore
I am not in England.

Or

If you smoke too much dope your reactions will slow down.
I have not smoked dope therefore my reactions will not slow down.

If you all vote Green you will get an inexperienced government.
We didn't vote Green therefore we will not get an inexperienced government.

If you eat chips you will get fat.
I did not eat any chips therefore I will not get fat.

The fallacious nature of these arguments is all apparent. Although it is true, for example, that one would get fat eating lots of chips it doesn't follow that you would get slim if you gave them up. One could substitute other fatty foods in place of the chips and the result may be as damaging.

Tip: Try to show that the consequences may be the result of some other action. i.e. one could get an inexperienced government formed by another party even if you didn't vote green.

This is a formal fallacy. See the section on the four basic syllogisms where examples of modus tollens and modus ponens express the correct forms of argument.

The Undistributed Middle
(A formal fallacy)

Examples

'In Buddhism there is no God. In Anarchism there is also no room for God. It follows therefore that all Buddhists are anarchists.'

This argument takes the form

All A's are C's
All B's are C's
Therefore All A's are B's

Or if we substitute the letters for real text we arrive at the following

All dogs enjoy running
All athletes enjoy running
Therefore All athletes are dogs.

Why is this a fallacy?

One has to demonstrate that because two or more things share the same property it doesn't mean that they lose their independence. Anarchists and Buddhists both agree that there is no God but they are still independent from each other on different grounds. For example Anarchists do not share with Buddhists their ideas on reincarnation.

Tip: The fallacy can also be explained by the realisation that the word 'some ' is suppressed in the argument. It can be written as this,

'all dogs (are some of the different creatures that) enjoy running.'
'all athletes (are some of the different creatures that) enjoy running.'

In this light one can easily see that the conclusion, 'all athletes are dogs' will not follow from the premises.

Relatively Speaking...

Examples

'A society's morals are only relative to its culture and development.'

'What is acceptable in our society will not be acceptable in another.'

'Everything is Relative.'

When Einstein developed and published his ideas on Relativity at the beginning of the 20th century, he introduced a whole new perspective on our understanding of the world. For hundreds of years humans had believed in absolutes. Physics had been dominated by Isaac Newton's works on Absolute time and Absolute space. Morality had been dominated by the Absolute word of God or the bible. Philosophy was dominated by a type of 'idealism' emanating from Hegal and Bradley.

This whole mind set was turned upside down by the likes of Einstein and Bohr (in physics), Russell and Moore (in philosophy). Further, the results from the Edwin Hubble telescope showed that the universe was not stagnant or absolute but expanding in size. Although this revolution in thought is generally welcomed, there was one interpretation of it that is not so welcome and still persists today.

This is the fallacy 'Everything is Relative.'

Why is this a fallacy?

When Einstein developed his General and Special theories of relativity he never said that everything was relative. He always held the view that there must be a base or benchmark from which one could begin and then everything was relative to that benchmark. If one did not have such a benchmark it would be impossible to compile any set of figures, tables or standards. Physics would cease.

Further the proposition 'Everything is Relative' has what is called a self-reference problem. If everything is relative then the statement 'Everything is Relative' is not itself absolute and could therefore be false!

Although physicists managed to avoid this problem, Relativism has been influential in the realm of Ethics and Cultural Anthropology. Subsequently, these views led to the school of thought that morality or moral rules can only be formed within individual societies, and would therefore vary from society to society. However, because relativity is the only criterion then individuals within society could also claim their own choice of morals. There can be no absolute guidance from external sources. This means that there are no benchmarks for making ethical judgements and one person's view is as good as another's.

The consequence could be that 'anything goes' and ethics is dead! This position is controversial and the issue is hotly debated in philosophical circles. I have only presented the briefest of sketches.

PART SIX - Formal Logic

Contradiction or Contrary

There is generally a good deal of confusion over what statements are contradictions and what statements are contraries. The principle of contradiction asserts that no statement can be both true and false.

Examples

'I eat potatoes but I don't eat chips.'
'I am a vegetarian that eats meat.'
'No one ever has the right to take another person's life but in some instances, capital punishment is justified.'

In both these statements the imaginary person asserts that x is true but then continues to assert that x is also false. This is a self-contradiction. In the case of the potatoes the person probably meant to say something similar to the following:
'I generally don't like potatoes unless they are fried.'

Because the person was sloppy in the formation of the statement the result is a self contradiction. Care has therefore to be taken. What of the case of taking a person's life? Is this just sloppiness? Let us try to reformulate the statement so as to avoid committing a self contradiction.

'No one ever has the right to take the life of an innocent person. Capital punishment can be justified only where a guilty person is concerned.'

Does the addition of the word innocent qualify the statement sufficiently to avoid committing a contradiction? Often we

103

consider a person to be no longer innocent if they intentionally take another person's life. (This doesn't apply to manslaughter.) It can be argued that capital punishment can be justly applied to those who might intentionally take another person's life.

Does this reformulation avoid contradiction?

It seems that it may do but there is a serious problem here. If we are to punish those who intentionally take another person's life, what should happen to the state executioner and the judge(s) that sent down the murderer? Should they now be punished also for intentionally killing another? Conceivably this would be the beginning of an infinite regress, with the new executioners now liable to execution themselves and so forth. This is clearly an unsatisfactory formulation of our original statement and we must therefore seek to clarify it further. Let us consider another refinement.

'No one ever has the right to take the life of an innocent person; capital punishment is justifiable in the case of and only in the case of the person who takes another's life without the full sanction of the law.'

This new refinement is beginning to look convoluted and is still not free from problems. Let us suppose the authorities execute a person for taking the life of an innocent. The executioner and judges intentionally take the guilty person's life and are protected by the proviso in the latest statement. The question now arises: are they protected in this action? Let us suppose that in later years more evidence come to light and the person x who was originally thought to have committed the murder now clearly didn't. Inconvertible evidence (if there is such a thing) shows that x suffered a grave miscarriage of justice being innocent all along. As x was innocent what should now happen to the people who tried and executed x? They intentionally killed an innocent, so should they now be tried? It seems that to protect the administrating authorities a further new proviso must be added to the original edict. This must include recognition of the fact that the prosecutors acted in ignorance but also on the best evidence available at the time. How one might reformulate this without further complications is an endeavour that I suspect is unlikely to succeed.

It is probably worth mentioning that there are other complications. The state and other states throughout the world usually have an ambivalent attitude towards the killings of innocents. In times of war, it becomes permissible to kill others (of the opposing side) in combat with impunity. In these circumstances the innocent and the combatants are not protected. When a stray bomb or missile accidentally destroys a hospital or nursery, there is no recourse to an action of manslaughter. These events become 'unfortunate' but permissible as a 'greater good' is said to be sought. Are these matters simply problems of consistency? It is not clear to me that one can formulate a non-contradictory phrase that allows some individuals to be killed and punished and others not. But I am open to suggestions. Lets turn to a less controversial contradiction.

'I am a vegetarian that eats meat.'

Clearly the person writing this statement does not understand what it is to be a vegetarian. This is a contradiction. A person is either a vegetarian or not a vegetarian.

What then are contrary statements or as logicians say contraries?
The following are examples:

a) Yesterday it was snowing throughout the Lake District.
b) Yesterday it was sunny throughout the Lake District.

These statements are contraries but why are they contraries and not contradictory? In this example both statements can't be true but they could both be false. It could have been raining throughout the Lake District. There are other alternatives to snow or sun. A contradiction occurs in the example of the vegetarian that eats meat because there are no other alternatives. A person is either a vegetarian or isn't a vegetarian.

Either a or not a.

Sub-contraries

There is another consideration when statements such as the following are said to be sub-contraries.

'Some actors are thirty years or older.'
'Some actors haven't yet reached thirty years.'

Sub-contrary statements could both be true but both cannot be false. Some actors could either be thirty or over, or some younger than thirty. There is no third alternative.

Why is it important to construct sound arguments?

The simple answer to this question is that if we do not reason

PART SIX - Formal Logic

correctly and take care to create sound arguments then it is possible that the consequences could be disastrous. This is particularly true if a politician fails to do this. Their conclusions and any subsequent implementation can have a tremendous affect on the lives of thousands. When they get it wrong many innocent people may suffer. As an example of this let us consider the reasoning behind the decision to go to war against Iraq. The following position, as far as I could see, was behind the thinking of the warring parties.

Saddam Hussein is preparing to go to war and is developing weapons of mass destruction that will cause much suffering. Either we attack now or Saddam Hussein will attack us later. If we attack now it will result in less suffering than if we attack later or if Sadam attacks us. Our justification for declaring war is to minimise suffering. Therefore we are justified in going to war.

If we convert these positions into logical form we will be able to evaluate the argument.

To begin we must construct the Modus ponens form. If p then q, p therefore q.

Argument 1

Premise1	If Sadam Hussein is preparing to attack us with Weapons of mass destruction then his actions will cause terrible suffering
Premise2	Sadam Hussein is preparing to attack us with Weapons of mass destruction.
Therefore,	Sadam Hussein's actions will cause terrible suffering.

Following this we are now in a position to construct a formal syllogism.

Argument 2

Premise i	All things that will cause terrible suffering are justifications for a preventative war.
Premise ii	(From above) Sadam Hussein's actions will cause terrible suffering.
Therefore,	Sadam Hussein's actions are a justification for a preventative war.

Although this is now a valid deductive argument, where the conclusion follows from the premises, it cannot however be considered a sound argument. The reason is because the following premises can all be considered false. In the aftermath of war it has come to light that;

Premise 1	Saddam was not preparing for war and was disarming.
Premise 2	Saddam was not about to attack his neighbours or western powers.

Further that,

Premise (i), is very questionable because we cannot be sure that a preventative war will not cause more suffering than that which it purports to prevent. An independent study reported that in excess of 100,000 innocent people were killed with many more suffering from injuries. Moreover, an escalation of terrorist violence has also occurred. One can also doubt if the prevention of suffering was the real motive for going to war; so this premise is also a red herring. Sceptics have always maintained that the real aim of the war was to secure the world's second largest oil reserve. With such unfounded premises one does not have to be a cynic to realise that an unsound argument resulted in injury and death to thousands.

PART SEVEN
The Threats

> *One of the necessary conditions for logical thinking is that all the information concerning the issue is available for consideration*

Audiatur et altera pars

'The other part should be heard too.'
Suppressed evidence

Examples

'One of the main achievements of this government is that during our term in office we have reduced income tax across the board.'

'The unemployment figures published today prove that Britain is back to work again.'

Of late this has become one of the most popular tactics, of

politicians in particular, to mislead the public. The error can be either a deliberate manufacture or an innocent act of assuming and not making explicit all the premises.

In the case above (from the 1980s) the direct Income Tax was reduced but National Insurance taxes and indirect taxes such as VAT were increased. The actual tax burden was actually higher since that government had taken office.

In the second example unemployment had fallen but newspapers reporting it forgot to mention (or didn't know) that the department of employment had re-classified some of those people seeking work. Although out of work they were no longer classified as such and hence a magical drop in the unemployment figures appeared.

Tip: The only thing one can do when the argument looks a bit fishy is to delve further into the facts and see if there is an alternative explanation for the conclusions presented.

(This can be a good exercise even if an argument doesn't seem that fishy)

The Threats to Logical Thinking

So far we have studied the numerous fallacies that we frequently encounter in our every day lives. We have also come to understand the nature of these fallacies and hopefully how we might avoid making the same mistakes ourselves. However, there is a greater threat to us all that can come from organised groups. This threat is not simply sloppy thinking or laziness but a deliberate attempt by these groups to undermine logical thinking. Unfortunately there are a rather large number of these groups, so my attention will be focused upon a couple of examples only. The objective is to illustrate the dangers we should all be aware of. I will begin at the end of a spectrum, which I believe is as far removed from logical thinking as one can get. This is the spectre of 'cults'. Most of us have heard of numerous Cults and realise that they take many different forms, differing in extremes. Essentially however they all employ the use of psychological methods to undermine logical thinking.

How do they undermine logical thought?

First we will examine some of the methods commonly used to render members gullible and devoid of logical thought.

1 Exclusion from friends, families and external media.

2 Acute peer pressure from new group. Strong approval and support for acquiescence but disapproval and ostracism for resistance.

3 Psychological intimidation. Where the member fails to adapt, the threat of possible poor health is strongly suggested.

4 Strong adverse emotional arousals. The member may be subject to humiliations, loss of privileges, social isolation, changes to social status leading to anxiety and intense guilt.

5 Self-confidence is undermined with the member becoming dependant upon the leader.

7 Obedience to Doctrine. The member or group becomes subordinate to the prevailing doctrine even if it runs contrary to experience.

8 Confession. Self-disclosure to group, often in public to past imperfections.

9 Mystical manipulation. Only the leaders can interpret the teachings or body of doctrines.

10 Prohibition of science. No facts are objective; the group or leader makes the 'reality.' The group can explain everything.

11 Language control. New vocabularies with parameters are enforced to prevent critical thinking. Everything becomes black or white.

These are the conditions for mind control in extreme form. None of the above would be conducive to independent thinking. As one looks through the list one can see that several of the pre-requisites for logical thought are outlawed. For example point 1 prohibits a member from gaining the facts or alternative viewpoints. Point 11 even restricts the vocabulary and parameters for thought. Our premises would therefore become highly dubious and our conclusions completely unsatisfactory in the least. Science is similarly restricted because an alternative set of facts would challenge the leader and the prevailing doctrines. Number 7 demands obedience. This means that our essential requirement to doubt or question things is conveniently curtailed. From the list one can also recognise that several modes of fallacy have been committed. Argumentum ad baculum is the fallacy that is committed when there is an appeal to force. This corresponds with the conditions of numbers 2,3&4 on the list.

The *Argumentum ad nauseum* is committed in point 6 where the attempt is to subvert logical thinking by repetition. Point 9 probably lays the foundations for the *Argumentum ad verecundum* to be committed as the leader is most likely to be an inappropriate authority. Point 11 commits the fallacy of Bifurcation when arguments are reduced to black or white alternatives. And so forth.

We can clearly see that the whole enterprise of a cult is at odds with what we have learnt so far. Their objectives are to trap and isolate the victims, remove their critical and questioning capacities rendering them dependant upon the leaders. This is usually enacted in order to either take financial advantage of the victim or to satisfy the desire of the cult leader's power.

These conditions are extreme and the anti-thesis of logical thinking. However, the conditions are not exclusive to cults. Many of these conditions appear in other organisations. I suggested that there could be a spectrum of positions, perhaps ranging from perfect logical thinking at one end of the spectrum to the extreme of cult behaviour at the other. Where do fanatical religions or political movements appear upon the spectrum? Are they far removed from the position of cults? (Perhaps I should mention that there probably is no perfect 'logical thinker.' It is however, a position that we can aspire too.)

PART SEVEN - The Threats

There is but one step from the grotesque to the horrible

How the political system thwarts logical thinking.

In our second example we look at how the behaviour of the governing bodies and the political parties undermine logical thinking. I have suggested that some political regimes may not be far removed from the behaviour of some cults in respect of their tolerance of free thinkers. Surely though democratic governments cannot be compared alongside these cults?

It is true that they are unlike totalitarian regimes but there are still aspects that are disturbing. Democratic governments vary a good deal in the amount of information that they allow the public to receive. Scandinavians can be very open and in Sweden even the minutes of cabinet meetings are available for public inspection. It is a very different story when one looks at the successive governments and administrators of Great Britain. Their affairs are shrouded in secrecy. Cabinet minutes and other official documents are withheld from the public for at least twenty-five years and in some cases for one hundred years! (Ironically politicians are surprised that electors become cynical about their behaviour)

The problem here for logical thinkers is that without the full facts at our fingertips we are unable to be sure that our arguments are sound even if we have reasoned in a valid manner. Our judgement of our leaders and administrators is incomplete and we are vulnerable to the 'spin' and 'gloss' so popularly employed. One might question this and argue that in a bi-partisan system the opposition should expose these inadequacies. Unfortunately the adversarial political system is not a system conducive to flushing out the truth but one of scoring party points and accommodating popular prejudices. This undesirable state of affairs is further compounded when such media as newspapers takes up the limited information released by governments. It is then filtered and re-interpreted, and re-spun to fit the political agenda of the owner or owners.

The Press, Watson, is a most valuable institution, if you know how to use it

PART SEVEN - The Threats

At the beginning of the book I suggested that the truth, however fragile, should be sought as a condition for logical thinking. This is proving difficult to achieve. So why do we allow governments of all persuasions to obstruct us? Why do we continue to buy newspapers that care little for alternatives and rarely employ reasoned arguments? One of the proclaimed benefits of a democracy is that we have the opportunity to shape our own destiny. However, for a democracy to be successful this has to be more than just a negative freedom.

Before we consider why we tolerate de-logical* forces an important distinction should be made.

We have referred to the 'Psychological' and to the 'Logical.' They are quite distinct. Psychology is concerned with the study of how we think and Logic is the study of how we ought to think. The former is an aspiring empirical science that studies the brain and how it affects our thinking and behaviour. Whereas, logicians assume that, providing we are not suffering from some form of brain damage, then we are capable of organising our conscious thoughts into logical forms. There can be tensions in some instances between these two modes with psychological factors pulling us one-way and logical factors pulling us another. The advertising industry has realised the importance of this distinction and devised all sorts of psychological ploys to induce us to buy their products. Most of the fallacies we considered are based on these ploys employing appeals to pity, violence, authority etc.

(*I have been searching for a word in the English language that represents the body of forces or modes of thinking that inhibit or subvert logical thinking. There does not seem to be such a word. I have therefore taken the prefix 'de' which means, 'indicating a reversal of process, or deprivation,' and added it to the word 'logical' which means, 'the science and art of reasoning correctly,')

Now that we are familiar with this distinction we can examine an illuminating experiment that demonstrated just how vulnerable we could be to inappropriate authority.

Obedience to Authority

Most of us think that our own minds and decisions are impenetrable from external forces. We believe it is others that are easily persuaded and manipulated by agencies, whilst we retain our autonomy. In the 1960s an experiment was devised to show that there was a big difference between how we think we will behave in a situation and how we actually do behave.

After the Second World War many questions were asked about the atrocities performed in Nazi Germany by people who normally would not entertain such thoughts and behaviour. Often the perpetuators claimed that they only performed these atrocities under duress and that they were only following orders. Explanations for this behaviour were sought after and an American, Stanley Milgram of Yale university, conducted a series of experiments that demonstrated just how vulnerable we all are to authority figures. These are his words to describe one of the earliest experiments.

In the basic experimental designs two people come to a psychology laboratory to take part in a study of memory and learning. One of them is designated a "teacher" and the other a "learner." The experimenter explains that the study is concerned with the effects of punishment on learning. The

PART SEVEN - The Threats

learner is conducted into a room, seated in a kind of miniature electric chair, his arms are strapped to prevent excessive movement, and an electrode is attached to his wrist. He is told that he will be read lists of simple word pairs, and that he will then be tested on his ability to remember the second word of a pair when he hears the first one again. Whenever he makes an error, he will receive electric shocks of increasing intensity. The real focus of the experiment is the teacher. After watching the learner being strapped into place, he is seated before an impressive shock generator. The instrument panel consists of thirty lever switches set in a horizontal line. Each switch is clearly labeled with a voltage designation ranging from 14 to 450 volts.

The following designations are clearly indicated for groups of four switches. going from left to right: Slight Shock, Moderate Shock, Strong Shock, Very Strong Shock, Intense Shock, Extreme Intensity Shock, Danger: Severe Shock. (Two switches after this last designation are simply marked XXX.) When a switch is depressed, a pilot light corresponding to each switch is illuminated in bright red; an electric buzzing is heard; a blue light, labeled "voltage energizer," flashes; the dial on the voltage meter swings to the right; and various relay clicks sound off. The upper left hand corner of the generator is labeled SHOCK GENERATOR, TYPE ZLB. DYSON INSTRUMENT COMPANY, WALTHAM, MASS., OUTPUT 15 VOLTS -- 450 VOLTS.

Each subject is given a sample 45 volt shock from the generator before his run as teacher, and the jolt strengthens his belief in the authenticity of the machine. The teacher is a genuinely naive subject who has come to the laboratory for the experiment. The learner, or victim, is actually an actor who receives no shock at all. The point of the experiment is to see how far a person will proceed in a concrete and measurable situation in which he is ordered to inflict increasing pain on a protesting victim. Conflict arises when the man receiving the shock begins to show that he is experiencing discomfort. At 75 volts, he grunts; at 120 volts, he complains loudly; at 150, he demands to be released from the experiment. As the voltage increases, his protests become more vehement and emotional. At 285 volts, his response can be described only as an agonized scream. Soon thereafter, he makes no sound at all.

For the teacher, the situation quickly becomes one of gripping tension. It is not a game for him: conflict is intensely obvious. The manifest suffering of the learner presses him to quit: but each time he hesitates to administer a shock, the experimenter orders him to continue. To extricate himself from this plight, the subject must make a clear break with authority.

The subject, Gretchen Brantt, is an attractive thirty-one year old medical technician who works at the Yale Medical School. She had emigrated from Germany five years before. On several occasions when the learner complains, she turns to the experimenter coolly and inquires, "Shall I continue? She promptly returns to her task when the experimenter asks her to do so. At the administration of 210 volts she turns to the experimenter, remarking firmly, "Well, I'm sorry, I don't think we should continue."

Experimenter: The experiment requires that you go on until he has learned all the word pairs correctly. Brandt: He has a heart condition, I'm sorry. He told you that before.

Experimenter: The shocks may be painful but they're not dangerous.

Brandt: Well, I'm sorry. I think when shocks continue like this they are dangerous. You ask him if he wants to get out. It's his free will.

Experimenter: It is absolutely essential that we continue....

Brandt: I'd like you to ask him. We came here of our free will. If he wants to continue I'll go ahead. He told you he had a heart condition. I'm sorry. I don't want to be responsible for anything happening to him. I wouldn't like it for me either.

Experimenter: You have no other choice.

Brandt: I think we are here on our own free will. I don't want to be responsible if anything happens to him. Please understand that.

She refuses to go further and the experiment is terminated. The woman is firm and resolute throughout. She indicates in the interview that she was in no way tense or nervous, and this corresponds to her controlled appearance during the experiment. She feels that the last shock she administered to the learner was extremely painful and reiterates that she "did not want to be responsible for any harm to him." The woman's straightforward, courteous behavior in the experiment, lack of tension, and total control of her own action seem to make disobedience a simple and rational deed. Her behavior is the very embodiment of what I envisioned would be true for almost all subjects. An Unexpected Outcome

Before the experiments, I sought predictions about the outcome from various kinds of people -- psychiatrists, college sophomores, middle-class adults, graduate students and faculty in the behavioral sciences. With remarkable similarity, they predicted that virtually all the subjects would refuse to obey the experimenter. The psychiatrist, specifically, predicted that most subjects would not go beyond 150 volts, when the victim makes his first explicit demand to be freed. They expected that only 4 percent would reach 300 volts, and that only a pathological fringe of about one in a thousand would administer the highest shock on the board.

These predictions were unequivocally wrong. Of the forty subjects in the first experiment, twenty-five obeyed the orders of the experimenter to the end, punishing the victim until they reached the most potent shock available on the generator. After 450 volts were administered three times,

the experimenter called a halt to the session. Many obedient subjects then heaved sighs of relief, mopped their brows, rubbed their fingers over their eyes, or nervously fumbled cigarettes. Others displayed only minimal signs of tension from beginning to end.

An extract from "The Perils of Obedience" as it appeared in Harper's Magazine. Abridged and adapted from Obedience to Authority by Stanley Milgram. Copyright 1974 by Stanley Milgram.

This experiment was copied and conducted worldwide producing very similar results. In one study however, over 85% of the subjects administered a lethal electric shock to the learner! Why did so many of the teachers not stop at the same point as Ms Brantt?

This rather chilling episode highlights how easy it is to be swept along by malevolent psychological forces.

Why should this be so?

After the experiments there was, and still is, a lot of debate in an attempt to explain our behaviour. With regard to logical thinking how should we perform in a similar situation? How can logical thinking help us?

Recognising and being aware of the dangers of obedience to authority is our first defence. Our second defence is our awareness of the psychological ploys or delogical forces that operate. Thirdly, we should be able to question and challenge the validity of such exercises. These defences, although they are necessary are probably not sufficient to protect us completely. I suspect that a measure of morality and confidence of action is also required and this goes beyond the scope of logical thinking. In some ways it is not too surprising that people did succumb to the wishes of the experimenter. From the moment we are born we are directed and controlled; questioning authority is not something we are taught whether at home, school or work. In fact we are taught to obey with varying degrees of punishment for those who do not conform. There are no lessons in critical or free thinking probably until one reaches university or chances upon an appropriate book. Fortunately we have an innate curiosity and this cannot be easily extinguished. The purpose of this book is to help develop it further.

PART EIGHT
Test Your Reasoning Powers

Are the following arguments valid?

Tip: remember the question is not concerned with the truth of the conclusion.

All women are compassionate
Anne is compassionate
Therefore Ann is a woman.

Nothing is better than wisdom
A crust is better than nothing
Therefore a crust is better than wisdom

Two plus two is four
Four is half of eight
Therefore two plus two is half of eight

If it rains the pitch will be soaked
The pitch is soaked
Therefore it did rain

If I get a good grade in my exams I will not have to work down the mines
I will not have to work down the mines
Therefore I will get a good grade in my exams

All pop stars drive tractors when the press is not present
Johnny Depp is a pop star
Therefore Johnny Depp drives a tractor when the press is not present

Some tigers are adorable
All adorable things should be cuddled
Therefore all tigers should be cuddled

All tigers are adorable
Some adorable things should be cuddled
Therefore some tigers should be cuddled

If it is Friday this is Paris
It is Paris
Therefore it is Friday

Either she will lock me out or send me to Coventry if I go home drunk.
I will go home drunk but she will not lock me out
Therefore she will not talk to me

What type of fallacy has been committed with the following?

1 Having thus conclusively shown that these figures are incorrect because of inaccurate sampling, I can only conclude that my estimate is the correct one.

2 Well, if you cannot find or name any errors in my proposal, it clearly does not have any.

3 There must be life on other planets because no one can prove there isn't.

4 The foresters are sawing down trees, so I should be permitted to cut down a few for my firewood.

5 Taking a car out of this whole car park full of cars is like taking a fish out of a whole ocean full of fish.

6 The Tsunami Disaster happened because God wanted to punish non-believers.

7 Please, lady, all I need to do is sell one copy of the 'Big Issue' and I can take my girlfriend to the cinema. If you don't buy one, she'll go with someone else. You were young and in love once, weren't you?

8 It must be a really good film all the famous actors have been to see it.

9 This play is performed in disregard of our sacred beliefs. We are entitled to block the entrance and threaten the actors if they continue with this insult.

10 It doesn't matter what you do, all your actions are making political statements.

11 There is nothing in the world that we can be sure of.

12 Our troops have a really difficult job, facing danger every day and risking their lives for our country. It doesn't help them if you keep undermining their efforts by calling on politicians to end the war.

Mental exercises
(for an individual or a group)

1. Choose a controversial topic
   (see below if you can't decide for a few tips)

2. Ask a friend or colleague what their views are? (for example, do they support nuclear power?)

3. Ask them how they justify their views.

4. Make a mental note of their reasons and later note them down in a piece of paper. Head it for and against in two columns.

5. Collect this information from several others, repeating the same question.

6. If they ask you your view, be non-committal, say you are thinking about it.

7. When you have a list of both for and against, read through carefully the reasons for and the reasons against.

8. From your awareness of fallacious thinking ask yourself if the reasons support the conclusion or not.

9. Add to the list any other resaons for or against you may think have been left out.

10. Look for contradictions between the two columns.

11. If someone has quoted facts, are they correct?
    Check them out.

Optional

12 Go back to a friend and say you know we were talking about... I'm still undecided on the issue, so and so (keep them anonymous) disagrees with you, give their reason, and I'm not sure what to think.

13 Your friend may be able to give a counter-response or reason. Note it down later.

14 Finally – read through the reasons again and highlight the ones you think valid.

Ask yourself

1 Have I learnt anything I hadn't considered previously?

2 Have I changed my view in anyway since the start of this exercise?

3 Do I feel more confident to come to an opinion?

(Don't worry if after all these you still are undecided, sometimes there is not enough information available to make a decision. There is nothing wrong with the standpoint, I have considered all the alternatives but still can't decide.)

Some suggestions for topics – fox hunting, abortion, road building/public transport, eating meat, nuclear power identity cards, giving aid, euthanasia, God made the world, alternative medicine, capital punishment, women's and men's rights, evolution, the latest war.
r

The Ten Commandments

(They are not really commandments but recommendations)

1 Thou shall try to discover the truth and not try to win an argument.

2 Thou shall judge an argument upon its merits.

3 Thou shall give good reason and evidence for thy beliefs.

4 Thou shall examine the arguments of others to see if they are guided by good reason and evidence.

5 Thou shall be honest to others.

6 Thou shall be honest to thyself.

7 Thou shall be prepared to say 'I don't know' when thou does not know.

8 Thou must postulate conditionals before making firm conclusions.

9 Thou must be prepared to question, including our most cherished opinions.

10 Thou must develop an appetite for 'finding out'.
.

GLOSSARY

Ad hoc
Used to describe a change in a hypothesis, often pejorative suggesting a change that is not based on any general principle. Something introduced for a particular purpose.

Affirming the consequent
A formal fallacy where the consequent is affirmed and not the antecedent.

Analogy
An alternative description or picture used to describe or elucidate a state of affairs.

Antecedent
The constituent that follows the if in a conditional sentence.

Argument
Where premises support a conclusion. Arguments take two basic forms, deductive or inductive.

Categorical syllogism
A type of deductive argument that must contain three terms and three categorical propositions. The proposition expressed in the conclusion is intended to follow from the other two propositions expressed in the premises.

Conclusion
A proposition or statement that follows from its premises.

Consequent
The constituent that follows the then in a conditional sentence.

Contingent truths.
Truths that are dependent upon our experience or observations. Empirical truths.
Truths that could have been otherwise: their denial is false but not contradictory.

Contradiction
A statement that must be false.

Contradictories
Where two statements are said to be the denial or negation of each other.

Contraries
Two related statements that cannot both be true but both could be false.

Deduction
A form of reasoning where the conclusion must follow from the premises. Where it does it is valid, where it does not it is invalid.

Delogical
Indicating a reversal of process, or deprivation of logical methodology. Forces or individuals that undermine logical modes of thought. Where the psychological is employed to replace the logical.

Denying the antecedent.
A formal fallacy. The antecedent is denied rather than the consequent.

Disjunction
A The connective 'or' employed in statements to indicate that one of the disjuncts must be true and the other false. (Example: He is either dead or alive.)
B The connective 'or' employed in statements to indicate that one of the disjuncts could be true or that both could be true. (Example; She is either on her mobile or driving her sports car or both.)

Enthymeme
Where premises or a conclusion remain unexpressed in an argument.

Ethics
The branch of philosophy that deals with moral issues.

Euphemism
A phrase that expresses a concept in a more pleasing manner. Sometimes misleadingly.

Explanandum
The phenomenon one is trying to explain.

Fallacy
Fallacies take two forms. (1) Informal. Incorrect reasoning. A rhetorical ploy. A form of argument where a (true or false) conclusion, is not supported by its premises. (2) Formal. Where the reasoning fails to follow the rules of deductive logic.

False analogy
A comparison that overlooks important differences among the items compared.

Hypostatisation
Treating an abstraction as if it were a physical object.

Hypothesis
A proposed explanation.

Hypothetical syllogism
Where a syllogism contains at least one hypothetical proposition or statement. Taking the form- if-then. Modern logic denies their status as syllogisms and refers to them as Modus ponens or Modus tollens.

Induction
One of the two major forms of reasoning or arguments. With Induction the conclusions are not deduced from the premises but nevertheless are probably true. The conclusions are said to be supported by the evidence and observations.

Inference
A form of reasoning where a proposition can be drawn from one or more other propositions.

Invalid
A form of incorrect reasoning in deductive arguments. However an invalid argument can be inductively strong.

Logic
The correct forms of reasoning. The study of arguments.

Modus ponens
A rule of inference that contains a hypothetical premise, which if true can support a conclusion. An argument of the form; If p then q, p is true, therefore q is true.

Modus tollens
A rule of inference that contains a hypothetical premise, which if true can support a conclusion. Similar to modus ponens but is distinguished by a negative premise and conclusion. An argument of the form; if p then q, q is not true, therefore p is not true.

Necessary condition
A prerequisite. In causal relationships for an event to occur particular requirements must be met or present. If p is a necessary condition for q then q cannot be true unless p is true, but it need not be true even if p is true.

Necessary truths
A statement that must be true. To deny this one would suffer a self contradiction, holding that a statement is both true and false at the same instance.

Premise
A piece of data or fact employed in a proposition in an argument to support a conclusion. A reason.

Proposition
A statement that is either true or false. Although its truth value may be unknown.

Reasoning
The subject matter of logical enquiry.

Rhetoric
An argument that relies on psychological devices to persuade. Not supported by good reasons

Sentence
A component of language that may express a proposition but may also perform other functions such as declarations, exclamations, interrogations etc.

Sophism
The art of rhetoric. Any fallacy of ambiguity.

Sound
A deductive argument is said to be sound when its premises and conclusion are true and the reasoning valid.

Sub contraries
Two propositions that may both be true but cannot both be false.

Sufficient condition
Conditions, which if present, are sufficient to explain or cause another condition. Example: 'If it rains her car will get wet.' The rain is sufficient to explain why her car became wet but it is not a necessary condition as her car could have become wet by other means, i.e. car washing.

Syllogism
Loosely, where two premises produce a conclusion in deductive arguments. It is an inference where one proposition, the conclusion is drawn from the other propositions, the premises. The propositions contain three terms one of which, the middle term must appear in both premises but not in the conclusion.

Symbolic logic
Also called modern logic. In modern logic deductive arguments are reduced to symbolic forms.

Tautology
(from the Greek tautos, the same) A proposition that must necessarily be true. A proposition that is true by definition. Circular.

Validity
Where a conclusion is correctly established from premises in a deductive argument.

ANSWERS

Page 125

Test your reasoning powers. Only two syllogisms were valid-Johnny Depp will drive a tractor and in the last test 'She will not talk to him'. All the other syllogisms were invalid.

Page 126

1 False dilemma or bifurcation
2 *Argumentum ad Ignorantiam*
3 *Argumentum ad Ignorantiam*
4 *Argumentum ad Hominem tu Quoque*
5 False analogy
6 *Post hoc ergo propter hoc* (Causal fallacy)
7 *Argumentum ad Misericordiam*. The Appeal to Pity
8 *Argumentum ad Verecundiam*
9 *Argumentum ad Baculum*
10 Every thing becomes nothing
11 Self-referential fallacy.
12 *Argumentum ad Misericordiam* or Red Herring

FURTHER READING
Books

These are the books on logic or critical reasoning that I have found most accessible.

Critical Reasoning: A Practical Introduction - Anne Thomson Routledge, an imprint of Taylor & Francis Books Lt Paperback - November 15, 2001

Critical Reasoning in Ethics: A Practical Introduction - Anne Thomson Routledge, an imprint of Taylor & Francis Books Lt Paperback - December 1998 (Anne's books are well written and the subject is clearly explained)

Introduction to Logic - Irving M. Copi, Carl Cohen Prentice Hall Hardcover - July 3, 2001 (A classic of the genre. Looks at informal and formal logic. CD also available with some editions)

Critical Thinking - Tracy Bowell, Gary Kemp Paperback - 288 pages (8 November, 2001) Routledge, an imprint of Taylor & Francis Books Lt; ISBN: 0415240174 (Good for formal logic, a good place to start)

The Logic of Real Arguments - Alec Fisher Paperback - 208 pages (14 July, 1988) Cambridge University Press; ISBN: 0521313414 (Slightly more advanced, looks at arguments from real life)

The Snake and the Fox: Introduction to Logic - Mary Haight Paperback - 512 pages (March 1999) Routledge, an imprint of Taylor & Francis Books Lt; ISBN: 0415166942 (A text book, , easy to follow with exercises. Well illustrated. Mostly formal logic explained)

Thinking from A to Z - Nigel Warburton Paperback - 176 pages (1 April, 2000) Routledge, an imprint of Taylor & Francis Books Lt; ISBN: 0415222818 (More like a reference book with good examples and clearly written)

Thinking Critically: Techniques for Logical Reasoning - James Hugh Kiersky, Nicholas J. Caste Paperback - 350 pages (November 1994) West; ISBN: 0314043527 (Thorough text book)

Critical Thinking: Developing an Effective World View - Gary Jason Paperback - 500 pages (November 2000) Wadsworth; ISBN: 0534573894 (One of my favourite textbooks. Very comprehensive, covers informal and formal logic.)

Straight and Crooked Thinking - Robert H Thouless Pan Bks. Paperback - May 1, 1970 (Out of print but still a classic. Examples are a bit dated)

Helpful books on Philosophy

Philosophy: The Basics - Nigel Warburton Routledge, an imprint of Taylor & Francis Books Lt Paperback - May 13, 2004

What does it all mean? - Thomas Nagel Oxford University Press, Hardcover - February 25, 1988

An Introduction to Philosophical Analysis - John Hospers Routledge, an imprint of Taylor & Francis Books Lt Hardcover - January 23, 1997

Sceptical Essays- Bertrand Russell Routledge, an imprint of Taylor & Francis Books Lt Paperback - February 2, 2004

Other invaluable titles

Obedience to Authority - An Experimental View - Stanley Milgram, Jerome Bruner (Foreword) Pinter & Martin Paperback - January 17, 2005

The Hidden Persuaders - Vance Packard Penguin Books Ltd Paperback - January 31, 1991

Other books by the author-

Who Holds the Moral High Ground?
By Colin Beckley and Elspeth Waters

Published by Imprint Academic

Are there any universal moral principles? Or is what counts as 'good' simply a matter of personal opinion? Are morals the product of a particular society or culture?

To what ethical criteria should modern secular societies defer? Can religion be considered a reliable authority? Are women any more virtuous than men?

Men have traditionally taken responsibility for moral authority, often to the detriment of women. Would a reversal of that gender dominance give rise to a more harmonious society?

From Buddhism and Christianity to Particularism, this book presents a history of morality and approaches to ethical problem solving. By demonstrating where each approach falls short in presenting an objective philosophy, it asks where that leaves us in the search for moral guidance. Are we facing moral nihilism? Or, can we create a new ethical consciousness from strands of what has come before?